Ocean-Born Mary

Ocean-Born Mary

JEREMY D'ENTREMONT

Charleston   London

THE
History
PRESS

Published by The History Press
Charleston, SC 29403
www.historypress.net

First published 2011

Manufactured in the United States

ISBN 978.1.60949.239.7

D'Entremont, Jeremy.
Ocean-Born Mary : the truth behind a New Hampshire legend / Jeremy D'Entremont.
p. cm.
Includes bibliographical references.
ISBN 978-1-60949-239-7
1. Wallace, Mary Wilson, 1720-1814. 2. Wallace, Mary Wilson, 1720-1814--Homes
and haunts--New Hampshire. 3. Londonderry (N.H.)--Biography. 4. Henniker (N.H.)-
-Biography. 5. Legends--New Hampshire. 6. Dwellings--New Hampshire--History.
7. New Hampshire--History, Local. 8. New Hampshire--History--Colonial period, ca.
1600-1775--Biography. 9. New Hampshire--History--1775-1865--Biography. 10. Pirates--
New England--History--18th century. I. Title.
F44.L8D36 2011
974.2'03--dc23
2011018585

CONTENTS

PREFACE

In his 1937 book *The Hurricane's Children*, popular author Carl Carmer wrote of the Ocean-Born Mary story, "When I heard all this for the first time, I thought somebody had just made up a fancy story for me that had few words of truth in it. But now…I'm not sure where truth ends and fancy begins. At any rate, many folks in New Hampshire love to tell this story on winter evenings before their birch-log fires, or on their porches on summer evenings when the stars are very bright above the mountaintops."

There's no doubt that the story of Ocean-Born Mary had its basis in a factual 1720 incident, but as it's now often told, it's laced with embellishments. Most writers on the subject have followed the famous advice given to Jimmy Stewart's character in *The Man Who Shot Liberty Valance*: "When the legend becomes fact, print the legend."

One of my goals as I began work on this book was to bring to light whatever nuggets of truth I might be able to surgically extract from the legends that have coagulated around the folktale. Lovers of romance and mystery might fear that this operation could kill the patient and leave us with a cold collection of a few names and dates. On the contrary, the truth of Ocean-Born Mary is fascinating in its own right.

The story's tangents provide us insight into colonial American history and the rich history of the Ulster Scots, or Scotch-Irish, who came to New England around the year 1720. As it turned out, my investigative trail led me to evidence that the real pirate captain who plundered Mary's ship may have been a much more impressive character than the fictionalized version who appears in most tellings of the story. I felt like I had unearthed pirate treasure when I arrived at my conclusions on the subject.

I also set out to examine the birth and growth of the more fanciful elements of the story as it's now usually told. A popular new twist on an old story can quickly supplant old versions as "the truth," particularly when you have a character like L.M.A. "Gussie" Roy, the man who engineered and capitalized on the revision of Ocean-Born Mary into a romantic ghost tale.

Gussie Roy was not an ill-intentioned man. In fact, his imaginative storytelling probably sparked a love of American history and antiques in some of his listeners. I would like nothing more than to go back in time to enjoy one of Gussie's spooky tours of his house in Henniker, New Hampshire, that he lovingly—but wrongly—promoted as the Ocean-Born Mary House.

I don't pretend for a second that this book will stop the story from being told and retold with still more embellishment. Facts are fixed, but folklore is not—it's a dynamic process that never reaches a final destination. I especially enjoy the New Hampshire historian J. Dennis Robinson's summing up of the Ocean-Born Mary story: "Drip, drip, drip, the legend pounds away at the facts, one drop at a time, eroding away the annoying bits of truth and keeping one more popular New England folk tale alive."

Humans are creative storytellers by nature, and the tales we tell help to define our culture. I enjoy a good romantic pirate story as much as the next person, and I'm not closed-minded when it comes to the paranormal. I believe, however, that we should try to keep our history, legends and ghost stories separate.

I'm far from the first person to point out that the bulk of what has been written about Ocean-Born Mary, especially in the last few decades, is either distorted or out-and-out fiction; J. Dennis Robinson, Andrew Rothovius, Alice V. Flanders and Fiona Broome, among others, have written well-informed articles on the subject.

Most of my conclusions are not very different from theirs, but it's my hope to flesh out the true story and chronicle the evolution of the legend in greater detail than what's already been written. This is a wonderful case study in the development of a legend over time.

I want to express my sincere thanks to everyone who provided pieces, large and small, of this fascinating historical puzzle. I particularly wish to thank Martha C. Taylor, Barbara Gratton, Jim McElroy and all of the kind people of the Henniker Historical Society, who were cheerfully helpful and provided much valuable material.

Thanks also to the Tucker Free Library in Henniker; Kendall Koladish at the Leach Library in Londonderry; David Lee Colglazier and Marilyn Ham of the Londonderry Historical Society; Wesley G. Balla of the New Hampshire Historical Society; Alden O'Brien of the Daughters of the American Revolution (DAR) Museum in Washington, D.C.; Marjory O'Toole of the Little Compton (RI) Historical Society; the Keene Public Library; the Portsmouth Public Library; Donna Gilbreth of the New Hampshire State Library; the Boston Public Library; the Dartmouth College Library; Fiona Broome; Bob and Terry Stamps; Dick and Anne Keigher; Tom Manchester; Phillip Seven Esser; James Garvin; Timothy Hughes; Lynn Bassett; Laurel Thatcher Ulrich; V'léOnica Roberts; and William Marshall, who helped solved the "Great Puzzle of the Dates." I also want to thank Jeffrey Saraceno, Ryan Finn and The History Press for helping to make the preparation of this book a pleasure.

And, of course, thanks as always to my wife, Charlotte Raczkowski, who has graciously (for the most part) humored my incessant babbling about Ocean-Born Mary for the past several months.

I remember learning about Ocean-Born Mary for the first time close to half a century ago from Keith Ringer, my childhood buddy back in Lynn, Massachusetts. He and his family toured the so-called Ocean-Born Mary House in Henniker several times, and I can recall his excitement about the purported ghost there. I dedicate this book to Keith's memory.

ONCE UPON A TIME

A Legend Is Born

In the year 1720, a group of Scottish emigrants from the northern part of Ireland left in a small ship bound for the New England coast. In the middle of their long and grueling voyage across the Atlantic, a pirate captain and his bloodthirsty crew boarded the emigrant ship.

The pirates plundered everything of value and threatened to kill the passengers and burn the ship. Suddenly, the pirate captain heard the faint sound of a bawling infant. Going below deck, the pirate captain found a frightened young woman named Elizabeth Wilson lying in a bed. Agitated by the terrifying events that had transpired, she had given birth to a daughter only minutes before.

The sight of the tiny baby girl melted the pirate's cold, cruel heart. He was so moved that he offered to spare the lives of all on board on a single condition: that Elizabeth would name her child Mary, after the pirate's late mother. Elizabeth agreed to this, and the lives of the passengers were spared.

Then, at the pirate captain's orders, a bundle of silk was presented to the young mother. "Your child," he told her, "should wear a dress fashioned from this fabric on her wedding day." The pirates departed, and the ship completed a safe voyage to Massachusetts.

The woman whose birth saved the lives of her parents and everyone else on the ship was known for the rest of her long life as "Ocean-Born Mary." She settled in the New Hampshire town of Londonderry, and for many years the residents of the town celebrated a day of thanksgiving on Mary's birthday, July 28.

Mary grew to be a tall, striking, blue-eyed beauty with long, flowing red hair. At the age of twenty-two, when she married James Wallace, Mary wore a lovely gown made from the silk that had been given to her mother by the pirate captain. Mary and James Wallace lived happily in the town of Londonderry, where they raised five children.

Some of the details vary from source to source, but the preceding is presented as a typical telling of the Ocean-Born Mary story as it's been related in many sources. Countless versions of the story have appeared in books and other

Nineteenth-century illustration of Mary Wallace's grave and the so-called Ocean-Born Mary House in Henniker, New Hampshire.

publications, dating back at least to the mid-1800s. The story's popularity owes much to the fact that it combined two elements that have perennial appeal: an ocean voyage with emigrants seeking a better life in the New World, and an encounter with pirates on the high seas.

Particularly from the 1920s on, the tale's fame has enjoyed a revival as thick layers of folklorish distortion have been heaped on top of the basic story—generous helpings of colorful romance, pirate treasure and a haunted house to boot.

In an effort to lay bare the truth behind the legend, let's begin with a review of the accepted facts, stripped of the fantastic embellishments that came later.

We know that James and Elizabeth (Fulton) Wilson, who had been married for about a year, voyaged to New England in the summer of 1720 on a ship full of Scotch emigrants who had been living in the northern part of Ireland. Elizabeth gave birth during the Atlantic crossing, and her baby was named Mary.

Mary went on to lead a long life as a beloved resident of Londonderry and Henniker, New Hampshire. She married James Wallace in 1742, and among their descendants were some of the most prominent residents of New Hampshire in the eighteenth and nineteenth centuries.

During her lifetime and in the centuries that have followed, she has been known as Ocean-Born Mary or Ocean Mary. Mary was described as tall, with ivory skin and bright blue eyes. She died in 1814, and her grave is located in a cemetery near the town hall in Henniker.

Those are the undisputed facts. There are other story elements that are difficult to prove but that *may* be true. During the 1720 voyage from Ireland, pirates boarded the ship, and Mary was born either just before or during the pirate siege. The pirate captain, upon discovering the newborn infant, was so moved that he decided to spare the lives of everyone on board the ship on the condition that Elizabeth would name her baby Mary, after the pirate's wife or mother. The captain also presented Mary's mother with a gift of Chinese brocaded silk, which was later fashioned into Mary's wedding dress.

The wild embellishments of the past few decades are mostly easy to disprove, as we'll explore later. Following are some of the story elements you're likely to encounter in recent versions.

Years after his encounter with the infant Mary, the pirate captain retired from the sea. He built a home on a hill by the Contoocook River in the New

Hampshire town of Henniker. When he learned that Mary's husband had died, the pirate invited the widow to live at his home as his housekeeper. One day, Mary was shocked to find the pirate captain dead outside the house. A rival pirate had come to look for a treasure that he believed might be hidden in the house, and in a struggle he had slain the captain with his cutlass. In the years since Mary's death, many visitors to the Ocean-Born Mary House in Henniker have seen her ghost arriving at the house in a phantom coach drawn by four horses, her fiery red hair streaming in the wind.

So they say.

The Ocean-Born Mary story begins in 1720, so in our examination of the facts it seems useful to begin with the accounts written closest to that time. While the tale certainly must have been popular in local oral tradition, the earliest-known published account is from the *Portsmouth* (New Hampshire) *Journal* of February 24, 1849, reprinted from the *Exeter News-Letter*.

The article began with the statement, "The following facts are related by an intelligent lady, and connected in direct lineage with the parties, now living." It continued:

> *In the year 1726* [sic], *an emigrant ship, laden with a band of Scotch-Irish adventurers, sailed for the American continent. While proceeding on their way across the broad Atlantic, they had the misfortune to fall into the hands of a band of pirates, who boarded the emigrant vessel, placing her unhappy inmates on board her own. Among the emigrants was a Mrs. Wilson, whose maiden name was Elizabeth Fulton; who, excited by the events of their capture, gave birth prematurely to an infant daughter. The captain of this pirate band, himself being a father, was induced to tender to the unfortunate lady every assistance in his power, allowing her to occupy the cabin of the vessel, granting her every comfort their situation afforded; and the pirates were constrained to release their hold upon the unfortunate adventurers, and suffered them to proceed on their voyage with all their effects, save a few muskets and some ammunition which the pirates retained. The Captain also gave her several valuable presents and relics, some of which are now in the hands of a namesake now living in Michigan, with the promise that the child should be named for the Captain's wife, Mary. The anniversary of this remarkable deliverance was devoutly commemorated as a day of annual thanksgiving by the early settlers during the whole of that generation.*

The article went on to recount the illustriousness of Mary's many descendants, who were "remarkable for their intelligence and enterprise." It concluded by quoting Mary herself:

> *In olden times when the early settlers were grouped together, and used to relate the place of their nativity, some would say it was on this side of the water, and some on that, but Mrs. Wallace would say, "Indeed, I was born neither on this side or that side o' the water, nor anywhere else on God's green earth" to the no small astonishment of the young ones.*

The fact that the wrong year is given for the event doesn't discredit the rest of the account; it could have been an error of transcription or typesetting. The fact that the account was written only thirty-five years after Mary's death, and that it is attributed to a relative of Mary, would seem to lend it credence.

Another early published account appears in Reverend Edward L. Parker's 1851 volume, *History of Londonderry: Comprising the Towns of Derry and Londonderry, N.H.* There are only two significant differences between Parker's 1851 description and the 1849 newspaper article, other than minor differences in wording. Parker provides a more detailed description of the presents given to Mary's mother, and he states that Mary was born on board the pirate ship. The pirates, wrote Parker, gave Mrs. Wilson "some valuable articles of apparel, among which was a silk dress, pieces of which are still retained among her descendants as memorials of her peril and of her deliverance." Interestingly, neither the 1849 nor 1851 account give a date, other than the year, for Mary's birth.

Parker (1785–1850) was pastor of the First Parish Church in Derry, New Hampshire, for about forty years. Derry in those days was part of Londonderry. According to Rick Holmes, former chairman of the Derry Heritage Commission, "In his Derry parish of 2,000 souls, he [Parker] personally knew the name of every child by sight." A contemporary wrote that Parker "possessed a mind of a high order, strong, and quick of apprehension." Parker had the reputation of being the best pastor in the state; he founded New Hampshire's first Sunday school and first temperance union.

Parker's book on Londonderry, published by his son a year after his death, is still highly regarded as an important and accurate early history

Edward L. Parker,
author of the 1851
History of Londonderry.

of the area. In addition, it's possible that Parker knew Mary herself; she
lived in Londonderry until 1798, when Parker was about thirteen years old.
It's believed that he knew Mary's daughter, Elizabeth Patterson, who lived
until 1833, quite well. He most likely knew Mary's sons, her grandchildren
and many other relatives and friends. In other words, Edward L. Parker's
account would seem to be reliable.

With the basic story established, let's begin a closer examination of
the details.

SOME HISTORICAL CONTEXT

The Ocean-Born Mary tale is one thread of the story of a remarkable immigration of a unique group of people to the New World in the 1700s. Before they left their home to start a new life, Mary's parents, James and Elizabeth Wilson, were among a large population of Scots living in Ulster, in the northern part of Ireland.

The Ulster Scots imagined the world across the ocean to be a place of religious tolerance and economic promise. One historian wrote, "Their imagined America seemed to offer economic opportunities they had come to expect, religious freedom they had never enjoyed, and the unity they had lost."

An estimated 200,000 of the people known as Ulster Scots immigrated to what would become the United States between 1717 and 1785. In the New World, they were, and are, commonly (and misleadingly) referred to as Scotch-Irish, or Scots-Irish. Author and U.S. Senator Jim Webb has suggested that as many as 27 million Americans have some degree of Scotch-Irish heritage.

Ulster, which occupies the northern third of Ireland, had seen a great influx of Scottish and English people in the seventeenth century. They began arriving in especially large numbers with the development of the organized colonization effort known as the Plantation of Ulster in 1609. The Scottish colonists who flooded into Ulster in the 1600s were primarily from southwest Scotland, and they were mostly Presbyterian. About 100,000 Scottish Presbyterians moved to Ulster between 1607 and 1690.

The primary purpose of the colonization was to stifle rebellion; the Gaelic people of the Ulster region had been openly resistant to English rule during the 1500s. The English defeated the Irish chieftains of the region in the Nine Years' War (1594–1603), which devastated Ulster.

King James I emphasized the need to inhabit Ulster, "being now depopulated and wasted, with English and Scottish men; and the carrying of men, cattle, corn and all other commodities from England and Scotland into the said territories."

James believed that the Scottish were suited to the adventure of resettling in Ulster. "The Scots are a middle temper," he wrote, "between the English tender breeding and the Irish rude breeding and are a great deal more likely to adventure to plant Ulster than the English."

Many of the native Gaelic Irish natives were forced from their homes with the arrival of the Scotch and English settlers, and the newcomers were plagued by thievery and attacks by the dispossessed Irish.

At the same time, civil wars were being fought in England, Ireland and Scotland, with the native Irish openly rebelling against the English and Scottish planters in the 1640s. The English took firm control of Ulster following a twelve-year war.

One of the most celebrated events in Ulster Scot history is the 1689 Siege of Londonderry. In 1688, James II, the Catholic king of England, was deposed by his Protestant daughter, Mary, and her husband, William of Orange, in the bloodless coup known as the Glorious Revolution. James incited his Irish supporters, and with the help of French troops, he captured Dublin.

In the spring of 1689, James's forces attacked the fortified city of Londonderry, a stronghold of the Protestant Ulster Scots. (The city's original name was Derry, but it was later changed by investors from London.) The residents of Londonderry refused to surrender. During the siege of more than one hundred days, about half the city's population of about eight thousand died, mostly of starvation. Others survived by eating dogs, cats and mice.

After 105 days, legend has it that a twelve-year-old named James McGregor fired a signal cannon from the cathedral tower; British ships had arrived. The attacking force was driven from Londonderry, and food was brought to the residents. James McGregor would later lead a group of Ulster Scots to Londonderry, New Hampshire.

The Truth Behind a New Hampshire Legend

There was a large new wave of Scottish immigration to Ulster in the 1690s, when many thousands of families fled the famine that raged in Scotland. By 1720, the Scottish Presbyterians made up the majority of Ulster's population. Six of Ulster's nine counties now make up Northern Ireland, created as a division of the United Kingdom in 1921. The Ulster Scots remain a major ethnic group in the region today.

A series of bad harvests in Ulster between 1714 and 1719 led to a recession in the linen industry and helped to trigger the wave of immigration to America. Increasingly high rent on land leased from the Crown was another factor, and the Ulster Scots were also compelled to pay one-tenth of their income to support the Church of England. Irish Catholics, with whom they had little in common, surrounded the Scottish Presbyterians in Ulster.

The immigration of Ulster Scots to America began in 1717, and they began arriving in large numbers by 1718. (A single ship, the *Eagle Wing*, had tried to sail to Boston in 1636 with 140 Ulster Scots aboard, but it turned back.) The ships that carried the Ulster Scots to America were not designed to carry large numbers of people; they were small and often overcrowded. There's some uncertainty about the numbers, but it appears that five or six ships arrived in Boston from Ulster in 1718, none larger than seventy tons.

Some of the Ulster Scots struck out on their own, but most stayed together in groups. The so-called Scotch-Irish were not the only people coming from Ireland; there were also Irish immigrants arriving in great numbers.

Both the Irish and the Ulster Scots were not always welcomed in Boston. Reverend Cotton Mather expressed his fears in his diary in August 1718: "But what shall be done for the great number of people that are transporting themselves thither from ye North of Ireland?"

An ordinance was passed in 1720 that directed "certain families recently arriving from Ireland to move off." In 1723, immigrants from Ulster were ordered to register with Boston's selectmen. The poverty of the new arrivals seems to have been at least as much a factor as religious bigotry in the anti-immigrant behavior of the New Englanders, who feared that the "confounded Irish will eat us up."

The Ulster Scots were soon carving out settlements in what was then the frontier of New England. Later waves of Scotch-Irish arrivals settled primarily in Pennsylvania, Virginia and the Carolinas.

Early homes built by Scotch-Irish immigrants in Worcester, Massachusetts, circa 1820. From *Scotch Irish Pioneers in Ulster and America*, by Charles Knowles Bolton (1910).

About fifty families journeyed in the fall of 1718 from Boston to Worcester, Massachusetts, which was then no more than an outpost in the wilderness. Hostile Yankees burned down that settlement's Presbyterian church in 1734.

Reverend James McGregor of Londonderry County in Ulster was a leader of the group of 1718 settlers that established the Nutfield settlement in New Hampshire. In Ireland, in March 1718, McGregor had cosponsored a petition to Governor Samuel Shute and the General Court of Massachusetts:

> *Praying that the Court would be pleased to grant unto them a convenient Tract of their vast Land, in such Place as they shall think fit, where they may without Loss of time, settle themselves & their Families, as over forty more Families who will come from Ireland as soon as they hear of their obtaining Land for Township; which they apprehend will be of great Advantage to this Country by strengthening the Frontiers & out Parts & making Provisions Cheaper.*

On the eve of their departure from Ireland a few months later, Reverend McGregor told his followers, "We must say farewell to friends, relations and our native land." He gave the following reasons for their emigration:

First, to avoid oppression and cruel bondage; second, to avoid persecution and designed ruin; third, to withdraw from the communion of idolaters; fourth, to have an opportunity of worshiping God according to the dictates of conscience and the rules of His inspired word.

McGregor sailed to the New World that spring with sixteen families aboard the brigantine (a two-masted, easily maneuverable sailing ship) *Robert*, arriving on August 4, 1718. Some of the group then proceeded north in the *Robert* to the Casco Bay region of Maine. The Casco Bay group suffered greatly from lack of food in the winter, but they were saved when the General Court of Massachusetts provided them with one hundred bushels of cornmeal. This group eventually reunited with McGregor and the other families.

After spending a brief time in Massachusetts, the families with McGregor eventually settled in April 1719 in an area of New Hampshire that was called

Drawing of a brigantine, similar to the typical ships used by the Ulster Scots to travel to North America.

Nutfield because of an abundance of nut trees (like butternut, black walnut, chestnut, oak, beech and hickory). Nutfield, the first inland settlement in the Merrimack Valley, originally consisted of a grant of 144 square miles, but by the time McGregor and his followers arrived, the grant had been reduced to about 114 square miles.

The first houses in the area were built of logs, covered with bark; the cabins were arranged around an open space called a common. The first homesteads were laid out in narrow farms of sixty acres each, arranged in parallel lines so that the cabins were not more than thirty rods (about five hundred feet) apart. The properties were set up in a "double range" on each side of Westrunning (or West Running) Brook.

A sawmill and a gristmill were established on the Beaver River by late 1719. The original log homes gradually gave way to more substantial wood-frame houses, some of them two stories high. Reverend McGregor's house was the first erected.

Two strongly built garrison houses were erected in case of Indian attack. Such an attack never occurred; in fact, the local Native American population was very small at this time. In his history of Londonderry, Parker wrote that one of the settlers was a man of "gigantic stature and fearless courage" named James Blair. It was said that on one occasion some Indians were preparing to ambush some of the settlers as they worked in a field, but they dared not

The first framed house in Nutfield. From *Willey's Book of Nutfield.*

shoot because they feared Blair and, according to Parker, thought him a god. This story is probably apocryphal, as most of the surviving members of the native Pennacook tribe had immigrated to Canada about 1677.

Bears and wolves were numerous and a constant danger. On one occasion, two settlers both named James Wilson (neither of them Ocean-Born Mary's father) followed a four-hundred-pound bear to its den. They waited for it to emerge, and one of the men shot it dead with a single shot. A third man who merely observed the operation was known to repeat the story of "how we killed the bear" so frequently that the phrase became popular in common speech.

Food was largely grown at the settlement or brought in from related settlements. According to historian Richard Holmes, the early settlers of Nutfield were indebted to local Native Americans for their survival in the first months of their settlement. When they had run out of their food supplies, an Indian known as Old Ezekiel took them to the Ammosceaq (Amoskeag) Falls on the Merrimack River. The falls teemed with eels, shad and salmon that were easily caught. Eels became a staple of the settlers in their first season in the area.

Reverend James McGregor brought some seed potatoes with him from Ireland, and he planted them in a common field in what is now the town of Derry. It's claimed that the first potato grown in the American colonies was grown at the Nutfield settlement. Some other states have disputed this, but the U.S. Department of Agriculture and the Potato Institute of America both agree that Nutfield is the birthplace of the potato in North America. The early settlers also planted apple trees, and apples became—and still are—an important local crop.

Reverend McGregor became one of the four original ministers of the colony, and he organized New England's first Presbyterian church. A house of worship was built by 1722.

About the time Mary's parents were journeying to the New World, some English settlers were also arriving in Nutfield. The English arrivals remained apart from the Scottish settlers, forming almost a separate colony that became known as the English Range.

We don't know precisely when Elizabeth Wilson and her infant daughter, Mary, arrived in Nutfield, but it was probably late in 1720 or early in 1721. In the coming years, the town and Mary would grow to adulthood together. By 1721, the population was 360 people. In all of New Hampshire in 1740, only Portsmouth, the state capital, had more people than Londonderry. By 1767, the population had reached 2,389.

Also among the Ulster Scots who arrived in Nutfield in 1720 was Archibald Stark. His son, John, would be born in the settlement in 1728. John Stark served as a major general in the Continental army during the American Revolution, and he gained fame for his exemplary service at the Battle of Bennington in 1777.

Mary Wilson was not the only child born at sea to Scottish immigrants to Londonderry in 1720. Elizabeth Arbuckle had the same claim to fame. She married Alexander Patterson; like Mary's sons, they later moved to Henniker, where Elizabeth taught at one of that town's earliest schools.

The first schoolhouse in Londonderry—a log building twelve by sixteen feet—was erected in 1723, and two years later the people voted to hold school for six months of the year. Little Mary Wilson may have attended school in the tiny schoolhouse, although it isn't clear if she had any formal education. One of the early teachers in the school, Eleanor Aiken, was among the first female teachers in the state.

On June 21, 1722, a charter was established for a new town called Londonderry, consisting of part of the Nutfield colony and named for the place in Ireland that had been home to most of the settlers. Also eventually carved from the original Nutfield settlement were the present city of Manchester and the towns of Hudson, Windham, Salem and Derry.

Much flax was grown locally, and the manufacture of linen in North America began here. The Nutfield settlers introduced the spinning wheel to their new land, and linens from Londonderry were considered New England's best. In the early days, the men did most of the weaving.

Edward L. Parker's *History of Londonderry* provides much fascinating detail of everyday life among the Scottish community in the early days of the town:

> *Their diversions and scenes of social intercourse were of a character not the most refined and cultivated; displaying physical rather than intellectual and moral powers—such as boxing-matches, wrestling, foot-races, and other athletic exercises…All this was done, not in anger, or from unkind feeling towards each other, but simply to test the superiority of strength and agility.*
>
> *The females, also, had their social interviews; but they were unlike parties of modern times, marked by cold formality, or ceremonious politeness,*

and by the exhibition and display of costly attire and finery. They would assemble from time to time at each other's dwellings, carrying with them the small wheel and the flax, and spend a long half day in social talk and diligent labor, combining in the happiest manner pleasure and profit.

Major earthquakes have been rare in New England in modern times, but there were some substantial ones in the seventeenth and eighteenth centuries. On October 29, 1729, when Mary Wilson was nine years old, an earthquake described by Edward L. Parker as "the severest ever known in New England" shook Londonderry. Twenty miles away, at Newbury, Massachusetts, the earth opened up in several places. "In many towns," Parker wrote in 1851, "numbers were awakened and hopefully converted, a reformation of morals was visible, family prayer was more generally attended, and great additions were made to many churches."

There are still reminders of the early settlement of Nutfield and Londonderry for those who look for them. One of the oldest standing structures in Londonderry today is the town pound, constructed by the town's farmers in 1730. The pound, simply an enclosure of stone walls with a gate, served as a place to hold cows that had strayed from their owners' property. The dirt path that passes near the pound was once Londonderry's main road.

The Morrison House Museum, run by the Londonderry Historical Society, is named for one of the original settlers from Ulster, John Morrison. The museum also includes a blacksmith shop and a barn. The buildings house artifacts related to the town's long and fascinating history.

Edward L. Parker summed up the proud legacy of Londonderry's first settlers:

Their faults—and faults they had—partly belonged to the times, but were more the effect of strong feelings without the advantages of early discipline. At the same time, they had in them the rudiments of a real refinement—warm, kind, and gentle feelings; and specimens of politeness were found among them worthy of the patriarchal age.

They have indeed long since passed away, but they have left their impress upon the generations which have succeeded them. Forever honored be their names, forever cherished their memories; not only by those who dwell on the spot planted by their hands, but by their numerous and widespread descendants; of whom it may truly be said, "The glory of children is their fathers."

THE REAL MARY AND
HER FAMILY

We know practically nothing about Mary's parents before their eventful voyage to New England in 1720. According to the *Genealogical and Family History of Western New York*, Mary's mother, Elizabeth Fulton Wilson, was born in Ireland in 1697. No source, it seems, provides the birth date of Mary's father, James Wilson. The same volume tells us that Elizabeth and James were married in Ireland sometime in 1719.

Shortly after James and Elizabeth Wilson arrived in Boston with their newborn daughter in late summer 1720, James Wilson died of an unidentified illness. *Genealogical and Family History* gives January 1721 as the month of his death.

It isn't clear if smallpox was to blame for Wilson's death, but there is evidence that points to that conclusion. *Willey's Book of Nutfield* tells us that some of the Ulster Scots who arrived in Boston in the late fall of 1720 were ill with smallpox and were not permitted to land. A smallpox epidemic would sweep Boston in 1721.

James Wilson had been granted a share of the land grant at the Ulster Scots' settlement at Nutfield in New Hampshire. After his death, his wife and daughter, referred to as "Eliz Wilson & mary her dater" in town records, were each granted half a share. It seems that the grant was further divided after James Wilson's death; a map in *Willey's Book of Nutfield* shows James Wilson's sixty-acre plot divided between Elizabeth and Mary, with a quarter-share each, and John McClurg or McClury, who received half a share.

The Truth Behind a New Hampshire Legend

By early 1721, Elizabeth and Mary were in Nutfield. It was undoubtedly hard being a widow with a small child to support in a strange and dangerous land, and it's no wonder that Elizabeth didn't remain unmarried for long. She was remarried on May 22, 1722, to Deacon James Clark (1691–1768), who had been born in Ireland. The historian Ezra Scollay Stearns wrote of Clark: "Living in a community renowned for mental activity and rugged traits of character, Dea. Clark was a foremost and useful citizen; honored in life and distinguished by descendants of character and ability."

James Clark's great-great-grandson, born in 1811, was Horace Greeley, the famous newspaper editor and politician. In a letter, Greeley once referenced his Ulster Scot ancestry:

> *I am indebted for my first impulse toward intellectual acquirements and exertion to my mother's grandmother, who came out from Ireland among the first settlers in Londonderry. My mind was early filled by her with the traditions, ballads, and snatches of history she had learned from her grandmother, which, though conveying very distorted and incorrect ideas of history, yet served to awaken in me a thirst for knowledge and a lively interest in learning and history.*

Elizabeth and James Clark went on to have five children, four boys and a girl. Elizabeth was only about thirty-five years old when she died on July 9, 1732; the cause of her death isn't known. Mary Wilson lived with her stepfather and helped care for her younger half-siblings until her own marriage in 1742.

James Wallace, another Scotch emigrant who would become Mary's husband, was about eight years her senior. James, the son of Thomas and Barbary (Cochran) Wallace, had come from Bush Mills in the Ulster county of Antrim, Ireland, to New Hampshire in 1732. That Thomas Wallace (1673–1754) was a man of some means is reflected in the fact that he once paid the unusually large sum of $100 for a male slave named Toney. (Census records show as many as twenty-five slaves in Londonderry/Derry in 1773.)

The historian Leander W. Cogswell described James Wallace: "He was a man of large hospitality, a genial man, a generous man, and one who, like many of his descendants, took great pleasure in the bestowal of gifts upon others." He was said to be one of the first to cultivate fruit in the area.

"Nothing was better known or appreciated than the flavor of his apples, plums, and pears," Cogswell wrote. In addition to being a successful farmer, Wallace was said to be an avid grower of rare flower varieties.

We know nothing about how they became acquainted or how their romance blossomed, but James and Mary were married at the meetinghouse in Londonderry, now known as the First Parish Church in Derry, by Reverend William Davidson on December 18, 1742. For her wedding, according to tradition, Mary wore a beautiful gown fashioned from the Chinese silk that was said to have been a gift from the pirate captain to her mother.

No details of Mary's wedding are recorded, but a look at the customs of the time helps us envision the event. In his 1851 *History of Londonderry*, Edward L. Parker described a typical wedding in the early days of the town, as related to him by one of the oldest residents:

The guests were all invited at least three days before the wedding, it being considered an unpardonable affront, to receive an invitation only a day previous. The bridegroom selected one of his intimate friends for the "best man," who was to officiate as master of the ceremony, and the bride likewise one of her companions, as "best maid." The morning of the marriage-day was ushered in with the discharge of musketry, in the respective neighborhoods of the persons who were to be united. This practice it seems originated in Ireland, in consequence of the Catholics having been, after the Revolution, deprived of the use of firearms. The Protestants, proud of the superior privilege which they then enjoyed, made a display of their warlike instruments on all public occasions. Seldom was a respectable man married without his sword by his side. At the appointed hour, the groom proceeded from his dwelling with his select friends, male and female; about half way on their progress to the house of the bride, they were met by her select male friends; and, on meeting, each company made choice of one of their number to "run for the bottle" to the bride's house. The champion of the race who returned first with the bottle, gave a toast, drank to the bridegroom's health, and, having passed round the bottle, the whole party proceeded, saluted by the firing of muskets from the houses they passed, and answering these salutes with pistols. When arrived at the bride's residence, the bridegroom's company were placed in an apartment by themselves, and it was considered an act of impoliteness for any one of the bride's company to intrude. When the ceremony was to commence, the "best man" first introduced the bridegroom; then, entering the bride's apartment, led her into the room, and, placing her at the right hand of her "intended," took his station directly behind, as did the "best maid." The minister commenced the marriage service with prayer; on requesting the parties to join hands, each put the right hand behind, when the glove was drawn off by the best man and maid. Their hands being joined, the marriage covenant was addressed to them, with appropriate remarks on the nature and responsibilities of the connection thus formed. Having concluded with another prayer, he requested the groom to salute his bride, which being done, the minister performed the same ceremony, and was immediately followed by the male part of the company; the females in like manner saluted the bridegroom.

The ceremony being concluded, the whole company sat down to the entertainment, at which the best man and best maid presided. Soon after the entertainment, the room was cleared for the dance and other amusements, "and the evening," remarks our aged informant, kindling at the recollection of by-gone scenes, "was spent with a degree of pleasure of which our modern fashionables are perfectly ignorant."

It has been written that the old records of Londonderry suggest that Mary's mother, Elizabeth, may have worn the same wedding gown for her 1722 marriage to James Clark before handing it down to her daughter. It has also been suggested that a granddaughter and great-granddaughter of Mary wore the gown on the occasions of their weddings.

Faded fragments of the gown are now on display at the Henniker Historical Society, the Tucker Free Library in Henniker, the New Hampshire Historical Society and the Leach Library in Londonderry, among other places. The fragments, including others that are owned by descendants of Ocean-Born Mary, all appear to match one another. Lynne Bassett, an expert on textile history, has said that the fragments look like they could authentically date to circa 1720.

Another swatch from the gown is housed at the Daughters of the American Revolution (DAR) Museum in Washington, D.C. Alden O'Brien, the museum's curator of costume and textiles, commented that the fabric is not typical for 1720, as fashionable silk brocades worn at that time were usually much larger-scale designs. But, he added, "Lighter-weight silks with

Fragment of silk said to be from Ocean-Born Mary's wedding gown. *Courtesy of the Henniker Historical Society.*

small-scale designs could also have been on the market. Indeed, looking at the silks in the very few early eighteenth century silk quilts that survive in Great Britain, one does find such light taffetas with smaller designs."

The Wallaces had four sons and four daughters, only five of whom—four sons and a daughter—lived to adulthood. According to a 1953 paper by Jim Newton, they had thirty-four grandchildren, and Mary lived to see nine great-grandchildren.

Not much is known of Mary and James's oldest son, Thomas, who was born in 1745, except that he married a "Miss Gregg" and served in the Revolutionary War. He was said to have taken part in the Battle of Bennington in 1777 and died soon after his return.

Robert Wallace (1749–1815), Mary and James's second son, was the most prominent of their children. Their third son, William (1760–1824), was also prominent in local affairs. James (1762–1795), the fourth son, was said to be "a valuable citizen during his short life."

The Wallaces' daughter, Elizabeth, married Thomas Patterson, from a prominent local family. Patterson was a lieutenant in the New Hampshire state militia. They had twelve children, six boys and six girls. Their son Peter represented Londonderry in the state legislature from 1819 to 1820 and later served in the New York legislature.

Mary Wallace knitted a pair of white stockings for Thomas Patterson to wear on his wedding day. According to family tradition, every one of the male Patterson descendants was to wear the same pair of stockings on the day he wed. The tradition was followed at least until 1966, when Robert Patterson wore the stockings at his wedding in Whittier, New Hampshire, with several other direct descendants of Ocean-Born Mary in attendance.

The stockings currently reside at the New Hampshire State Historical Society in Concord, along with towels and a sheet that are also said to have been made by Mary Wallace. According to Laurel Thatcher Ulrich in *The Age of Homespun*, the stockings were likely knitted from slave-grown cotton brought from the West Indies. The creation of the towels is recounted in an

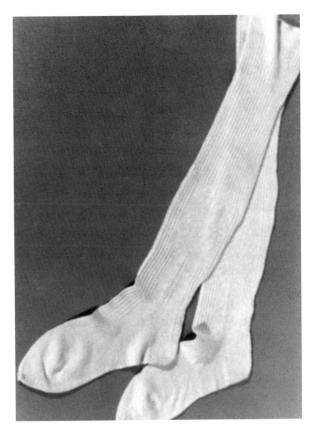

These stockings are said to have been knitted by Mary Wallace for her daughter's husband to wear at his wedding. *Courtesy of the New Hampshire Historical Society.*

attached description—Mary spun the warp, and her daughter, Elizabeth, spun the weft, while Peter Patterson (father of Thomas) did the weaving.

Three of the Wallace brothers married three sisters (Jeanette, Hannah and Anna Moore of Londonderry's "English Range"), and the three couples all settled in Henniker, New Hampshire. Henniker, billed as "the only Henniker on Earth," was a new town that had been carved out along the hilly, picturesque banks of the Contoocook River. Governor John Wentworth had named the town for his friend, the wealthy London merchant John Henniker, in 1768.

Robert Wallace and his wife, Jeanette Moore, moved to Henniker in the year following their marriage in 1776. The couple had eight children, four of whom died in childhood. There was much tragedy in the Wallace family; one of Robert Wallace's sons who reached adulthood, William, was killed while blasting rocks in 1813.

Robert's handsome Georgian-style home in Henniker, built 1784–86, still stands. It's known widely as the Ocean-Born Mary House, in spite of the fact that Robert's mother never lived in it.

Robert Wallace became one of Henniker's most illustrious and prosperous citizens. He apparently made a great deal of money through his work as a lawyer, in addition to land speculation, money lending and the raising of cattle and horses.

Leander W. Cogswell wrote of Robert Wallace:

> *He at once became one of the leading men of the town; and during the dark hours of the Revolution his voice and his counsel were ever in request. To him, perhaps, more than to any other one person, was the town indebted for the promptness with which all demands upon it, whether for men or for supplies, were met. Dec. 6, 1782, he was chosen to represent this town and Hillsborough for a term of two years in the legislature of the state, and was reelected in 1784 for another two years. He was selectman from 1779 to 1791 inclusive, save three years, and was chairman of the board ten years. He was one of the councillors of the state from 1788 to 1803, a period of fourteen years. In 1791 he was a delegate from this town to the convention to frame a constitution for the state. In this convention he was chosen one of a committee often to take into consideration the constitution that had been prepared at that session, and to prepare and report, at an adjourned*

session, the alterations and amendments to be submitted to the people. In that convention were some of the ablest men of the state; and the position to which Mr. Wallace was appointee was a testimony of the high regard in which he was held by the members of that convention. In 1803 he was appointed a judge of the Court of Common Pleas for Hillsborough county, to which this town still belonged, a position beheld until 1813.

He was the possessor of a large and highly-cultivated estate in the southwest part of the town, upon which he erected one of those noble mansions of the olden time, around whose hearthstone every one was made welcome, and whose hospitality was unbounded.

Although in public life continually for nearly a third of a century, his home and its inmates were never forgotten. There his brightest traits of character were shown, and his best humor, with his broad Scotch accent was exhibited. No one was turned from his door, but all alike were welcome. As he rode to church, and upon other occasions, in almost royal style, everybody did him homage, and all received from him a pleasant recognition in return. At his death the whole population of Henniker were sincere mourners, for the town had lost one of its most upright and honored citizens.

Mary and James Wallace's third son, William, raised horses, made spinning wheels, taught school (he was "beloved by his pupils," according to Cogswell), worked as a surveyor, served as justice of the peace and selectman and served a term in the state legislature. He is credited with the creation of the first good map of Henniker. "No man in the town had a larger influence in its affairs and in settling private matters than had 'Squire Wallace,' as he was known for so many years," Cogswell wrote.

William, a giant at six foot, four inches and 240 pounds, was described by Cogswell:

Possessed of great reasoning powers and superior judgment, he was always actuated by high moral principles and honest, manly purposes in all his dealings. In his conversation he was very fluent and affable, and in public was always listened to with marked attention. He lived a life of usefulness, and was much endeared to all who knew him as a man of integrity, and purity of principle and purpose.

William's house was a little over a mile away and slightly less ostentatious than the home of his brother, Robert. When asked why his home was built with such high ceilings, Robert once replied, "One reason is, my brother William is very tall, and as I want him to visit me, I have the rooms made high."

Mary's husband, James Wallace, died at the age of seventy-nine on October 30, 1791, just a year shy of their fiftieth anniversary. James Wallace was remembered by a friend as a "kind-hearted man, and a man of prayer." In his will, he left his farm to his grandson, James (son of the late Thomas Wallace, Mary and James's oldest son).

To Mary, James left "the income of the whole of my real estate during her natural life and also the use of the whole of my household furniture and the whole of the said household to be at her disposal at her death."

James Wallace was buried at the Old Hill Graveyard in Londonderry. One of Mary and James's daughters, Mary, who died at the age of eight in 1760, is memorialized on the same gravestone.

The grave of Mary's husband, James Wallace, at the Old Hill Graveyard in Londonderry, New Hampshire. *Photo by Jeremy D'Entremont.*

Also buried at James Wallace's grave site in Londonderry is a daughter, Mary, who died in 1760. *Photo by Jeremy D'Entremont.*

Mary was seventy-one when her husband died, not a "still beautiful widow of middle age with five young children," as she was described in Marion Lowndes's book *Ghosts that Still Walk: Real Ghosts of America.* Leander W. Cogswell, in his book *The History of the Town of Henniker,* wrote the following description of Mary Wallace in her later years:

> *She was remembered as being quite tall, resolute, and determined; of strong mind, quick of comprehension, with a strong brogue, and full of humor. She was florid of complexion, bright eyed, and elegant in her manners to the last of her life. Her younger life experience was wonderful in toils and hardships; but her last years were sunny and happy.*

An 1898 article by Ida G. Adams provides a similar description, the only addition being that Mary was "sharp in her conversation." J. Warren Thyng's 1906 article describes Mary as "a woman symmetrically tall, with light hair, blue eyes and florid complexion, together with a touch of the aristocracy of nature and a fine repose of manner in her energetic, determined and kindly ways."

William became his mother's caregiver in her last years. In July 1798, just before her seventy-eighth birthday, Mary left Londonderry to live with her William in Henniker. William recorded in his daybook that his mother arrived at his home on July 6, 1798, and the census records of 1800 and 1810

Ocean-Born Mary's grave in Henniker, New Hampshire. *Photo by Jeremy D'Entremont.*

indicate that Mary was living in his home. The family's farm in Londonderry was sold to Captain William Gage.

A preserved receipt from 1804, from a Henniker doctor, bears the words, "From son William, payment for treatment of his mother," adding further credence to the fact that William was the primary caregiver for his mother in her elderly years.

Mary died on February 13, 1814, at 6:00 p.m. The notoriety of Ocean-Born Mary had apparently faded, as evidenced by the brief note in the *Farmer's Cabinet* newspaper: "DIED: In Henniker, on the 13th of Feb. last, widow: Mary Wallace, aged 94."

Mary was buried in William's lot in the cemetery near the present Henniker Town Hall. The gravestone is inscribed, "In Memory of Widow Mary Wallace, who died Feb'y 13, A.D., 1814, in the 94th year of her age." A small marker has been added to the grave site, bearing the words, "Ocean-Born Mary." Although she only lived in Henniker for the last sixteen years of her life, Mary Wallace remains one of the most famous residents in the town's history.

On January 30, 1815, less than a year after his mother's death, Robert Wallace died after a fall from his horse outside his home. Robert is buried down the road from his mother in Henniker's First Burial Yard. A glowing tribute was printed in a local newspaper:

> *It is but a tribute justly due to his memory to say, that, in addition to an uncommon fidelity and a fund of good sense, he possessed an excellent natural disposition. Always happy in the felicity of others and wounded in their woes, after justifying the confidence of his fellow citizens for many years, as representative, senator, councillor, and judge, in succession, he bid adieu to the world in calm resignation to the will of Heaven, and with an unsullied reputation. In his death the state has lost a worthy citizen; religion,*

The grave of Robert Wallace is located in the First Burial Yard in Henniker. *Photo by Jeremy D'Entremont.*

a friend; his wife, a kind-hearted husband; his children, an indulgent father; and his connections, an affectionate relative.

The life of William Wallace, father of eleven children, was also cut short by an accident. He died at sixty-four in 1824 from injuries suffered when he was cutting down a tree. William's grave is next to his mother's in Henniker.

The illustriousness of Mary's descendants continued through to the twentieth century. Robert's oldest son, James, was the first person to operate a "public house," or inn, in Henniker, and he was said to possess "the same uprightness of character that distinguished his father."

Robert's great-grandson, Robert Moore Wallace, became chief justice of New Hampshire, 1901–10. A historian wrote of him, "From such a resolute, intelligent and distinguished ancestry, strange would it be if aught but the choicest fruit had ripened on this family tree. The lineage from which Judge Wallace came called for a man, and he appeared, clad in the armor of righteousness and power." Robert Moore Wallace's son, Robert

Robert Moore Wallace, chief justice of New Hampshire 1901–10 and the great-great-grandson of Ocean-Born Mary. *Courtesy of Phillip Seven Esser.*

Right: Elizabeth Wallace, direct descendant of Ocean-Born Mary and the last of her branch of the Wallace name. *Courtesy of Bachrach Studios, New York, and Elizabeth's son, Phillip Seven Esser.*

Below: The Bible once owned by Mary Wallace. *Courtesy of the Henniker Historical Society.*

Burns Wallace, was the head of sales for the New England Division of Bethlehem Steel.

A Bible that was printed in Scotland in 1700 and owned by Mary Wallace, was, for many years, in the possession of Mary Ann Wood of Hillsboro, New Hampshire. It was said that Mary Wallace read from the Bible, which is the only indication we have that she knew how to read. It isn't clear that she ever learned to write; she signed her name "by mark."

The Bible was passed down to Wood's daughter, Mary L. Cote, who died in 1937. For many years, one girl in each generation descended from Mary Wallace's daughter, Elizabeth Patterson, was named Mary; Mary Cote was said to be the last in that line.

THE LEGEND GROWS

There doesn't appear to have been much written about Ocean-Born Mary between the mid-1800s and the late 1800s, when the story was revived in several national publications. Edward L. Parker's 1851 account was reprinted almost word for word in an 1855 book, *The Life of Horace Greeley*. There was also an intriguing paragraph in the July 8, 1869 edition of the *Farmer's Cabinet* that described some "antiquarian curiosities" that were displayed at an exhibition in Derry, New Hampshire.

Among the curiosities were "plates brought over from Ireland in 1720, by emigrants, who, soon after embarking, were captured by a pirate ship." The article continued, "Soon after the capture, a daughter was born to one of the emigrants, on board the pirate ship, and the plates were given to her. She was the ancestress of Hon. G.W. Patterson, the President of the day."

In addition to the mention of the plates, the item is notable because it states that Mary was born aboard the pirate ship, rather than on the emigrant ship, something that's not a typical detail of the story.

A version of the story published in 1876 as part of the Patterson family's genealogy in *A History of Livingston County, New York* states that Mary was born prematurely while the pirate encounter was underway. The same detail appeared in the 1849 account but has rarely been included in later telling: "The vessel on which her parents had taken passage for this country, was captured in mid-ocean by a pirate, and while a prisoner the mother gave premature birth to this child."

The 1876 account also adds the detail that jewelry was presented to Mary's mother, along with the silk, by the pirate captain.

Mary's story was told again in Leander W. Cogswell's 1880 *History of the Town of Henniker*. Like other tellings of the Ocean-Born Mary tale published in the late 1800s, Cogswell added few details to the story as it was already known.

Ida G. Adams's telling of the story, "An Historical Romance," appeared in *Granite State* magazine in July 1898. Adams described the immigrants' voyage as "rough and stormy." She presented the following detail and dialogue describing the pirate encounter:

> *While the fate of the vessel was still undecided, and the officers and men lay helpless and bound on deck, the young wife of James Wilson, one of the Scotch-Irish passengers, gave birth to a child.*
>
> *The pirate captain, finding the poor, young mother, helpless and white with terror, inquired why she was lying on her bed. Too frightened to speak, she turned down the covers which concealed the little stranger. The hardened heart of the pirate chief was touched, and the thought of his own little ones at home awoke the natural tenderness in his nature, which a life of crime and desperate deeds had not yet wholly extinguished.*
>
> *"Is it a boy or girl?" he questioned.*
>
> *"A girl," was the faint reply.*
>
> *For a moment the man stood gazing at mother and child, while the passions of cruel greed and despotic love of power strove against his better impulses of chivalrous honor and pitying humanity. At last the struggle ended, and the father's heart overcame the pirate's greed. With softened voice he again addressed the mother:*
>
> *"On one condition I will spare this ship and cargo and the lives of all on board, and that is, that you will allow me to name your child."*
>
> *Elizabeth Wilson, filled with joy and gratitude at the prospect of so simple a way of deliverance, quickly gave her consent.*
>
> *"I will call her Mary," said the pirate, "in honor of my wife and the mother of my own little daughter at home."*
>
> *In reply to the mother's grateful thanks for his clemency, the pirate captain answered: "It is I who owe a debt of gratitude to you, for you have saved me from having one more sin on my soul."*

The Truth Behind a New Hampshire Legend

With that he left her, and immediately gave orders to his men to unbind their victims and prepare to leave the ship.

Before he left, however, the pirate chief returned to Elizabeth Wilson and gave her some valuable jewels and a beautiful piece of silk, with the request that the latter should be kept for her daughter Mary's wedding-gown.

A poem, "Mary Wilson Wallace," by Mrs. Arthur C. Graves, was written in 1902 and appeared in *Granite Monthly*. The poem describes the events of the story in a highly romantic fashion.

Here are the first two verses:

"Elizabeth," spake James Wilson,
To his bride of only a year,
"Could you leave our home in Ireland
With scarce a regretful tear?
We are young with our lives before us,
Each of us brave and true,
Shall we go to seek our fortunes
Far away o'er the ocean blue?"

"An emigrant ship is coming,
A ship of the very best class;
Our neighbors and friends are going,
Shall you and I go, my lass?"
"My Jamie," the young wife answered,
"You surely know what is best,
So when the good ship sails away,
We will go along with the rest."

It promoted the story to a wider audience, but Graves's poem didn't include any new or noteworthy ingredients. The final two verses, however, may have contributed to the confusion about where Ocean-Born Mary lived after moving from Londonderry to Henniker.

A hundred and seventy [sic] *years ago,*
In good Londonderry town,

Ocean Mary was married;
The pirate's gift her gown.
Four sons were born to Mary,
In a town where hills abound,
One built by far the grandest house
In all the country around.

There in the town of Henniker
Ocean Mary lived many years;
Having her share with others
Of sweet happiness and tears.
And there in a quiet church yard
Her body is laid away,
Safe from the perils of sea or land,
Awaiting the judgment day.

This is ambiguous; it could be easily inferred that Mary lived with her son Robert, who was the builder of the "grandest house" in Henniker. In reality, she spent her last years living with her son William at his home in Henniker.

An article titled "The Romance of 'Ocean Mary,'" written by J. Warren Thyng, was published in *Granite State* magazine in June 1906. Thyng got some of the details wrong, such as the name of Mary's husband, but his telling of the story is one of the best ever in terms of its dramatic quality. The entire article is included at the end of this book.

Thyng wrote that the ship that brought Mary and her parents to the New World was "in many respects vastly superior to others in her class in those times." His source for this assertion is unknown. Thyng's description of the ship's departure from Ireland is picturesque: "Out through Lough Foye, past Inishowen Head and far beyond Giant's Causeway, with favoring winds, sailed the fated ship."

Thyng wrote that "certain fragmentary accounts" hinted of "a protracted calm and following storm of such violence that the vessel was driven from her course." He stated that the pirate attack came about one-third of the way into the voyage.

Thyng's account of the pirate encounter is very similar to Adams's, but he left the meaning to the pirate of the name "Mary" a mystery:

The Truth Behind a New Hampshire Legend

Then the rough old robber came nearer still and took up the tiny, unresisting hand of the baby. "Mary," was the name the woman heard him speak. There were other words, but spoken so low she could not hear. Only his Maker and his own heart knew, but when the child drew its hand away the mother saw a tear on the pink fingers.

One of the most important occurrences that brought the Ocean-Born Mary story—or at least a highly fictionalized version of it—to wider audiences was the publication of Lois Lenski's book *Ocean-Born Mary* in 1939.

Lenski (1893–1974), the Ohio daughter of a Prussian immigrant, was a very prolific and popular author and illustrator of young adult fiction. During a career that spanned more than fifty years, she wrote and illustrated nearly one hundred of her own books, and she illustrated about fifty books for other authors.

Ocean-Born Mary was one of Lenski's many regional novels about children in the United States, a list that included *Strawberry Girl*, a book about a girl in Florida that earned Lenski the Newbery Medal for distinguished contribution to American literature for children.

Lenski's book has little relation to the true story of Mary Wilson Wallace, and Lenski never claimed otherwise. In an afterword, she quoted Edward L. Parker's account of the story. She described the so-called Ocean-Born Mary House in Henniker and made the mistake of saying that Mary spent the latter part of her life there. She repeated some dubious ghost stories and tales of pirate treasure. To her credit, after relating the highly questionable parts of the story, Lenski wrote, "It is difficult to say how much truth there is in these stories."

The bulk of Lenski's book is fictional. Lenski has Mary living in Portsmouth, New Hampshire, for sixteen months at about the age of twelve. The voyage in 1720 is mentioned only in retrospect and is not a focus of the novel. Instead, Lenski chose to paint a portrait of life in a New England seaside town in the colonial period from the viewpoint of a little girl who just happened to have been born at sea.

The nearly four-hundred-page book is colorful and picturesque and is full of rich detail and historical nuggets. The book is a wonderful source for anyone who wants to learn about Portsmouth in 1732, but it's not worth mentioning as a source on the true story of Mary Wilson Wallace.

Illustrations by Lois Lenski from her 1939 book *Ocean-Born Mary*.

In Lenski's novel, the pirate captain of the story is identified as Philip Babb. Lenski turns him into a respectable sea captain living in Portsmouth. The character is described as "a large, bulky man, wearing a long, black, curled wig," with a "long, black broadcloth cape and a red sash draped from shoulder to hip." In Lenski's version, Mary is named for Babb's late sister, rather than the pirate's mother or wife as usually cited.

This appears to be the first time the name Philip Babb appears in relation to the Ocean-Born Mary story. The name is now enmeshed in the legend, as a number of books and websites have stated as absolute fact that the pirate captain who boarded Mary's ship was Philip Babb.

There really was a Philip Babb; he lived in the seventeenth century on Hog Island (now Appledore Island), in the Isles of Shoals, off the New Hampshire seacoast. Records show that he was appointed constable for the Isles of Shoals in 1653. Legend has it that Babb was also a pirate and that his ghost haunts Appledore Island today. Celia Thaxter wrote in her 1873 book *Among the Isles of Shoals*:

> *There is a superstition among the islanders that Philip Babb, or some evil-minded descendant of his, still haunts Appledore, and no consideration would induce the more timid to walk alone after dark over a certain shingly beach on that island, at the top of a cove bearing Babb's name, for there the uneasy spirit is oftenest seen. He is supposed to have been so desperately wicked when alive, that there is no rest for him in his grave. His dress is a coarse, striped butcher's frock, with a leather belt, to which is attached a sheath containing a ghostly knife, sharp and glittering, which it is his delight to brandish in the face of terrified humanity.*

Philip Babb, who was born in 1619, obviously couldn't have been the pirate captain who boarded Mary's ship; he would have been 101 in 1720. He had a son with the same name, born in 1666. Some have theorized that the younger Babb was the pirate of the Ocean-Born Mary story.

That theory holds no water, either, based on Lenski's own disclaimer. In the afterword of *Ocean-Born Mary*, Lenski wrote: "My story is, of course, entirely fiction…Appledore Island has for two centuries been haunted by the specter of Philip Babb or "Old Babb," who is said to have been a pirate, one of Captain Kidd's men…I have taken the liberty of appropriating his name, but the character that I have built up, is imaginary."

Another popular book that spread a distorted version of the Ocean-Born Mary story was the 1941 *Ghosts that Still Walk* by Marion Lowndes. Lowndes claimed that the ghost of Ocean-Born Mary had been seen by at least seven people and sensed by many more.

The writings of the prolific New England historian and storyteller Edward Rowe Snow (1902–1982) also played a role in popularizing the story. Snow's many books were perennial regional bestsellers from the 1930s to the 1980s. He related the Ocean-Born Mary story in his 1957 book, *Legends of the New England Coast*, and his 1974 book, *Supernatural Mysteries and Other Tales*.

A 1971 book, *The Flaming Ship of Ocracoke and Other Tales of the Outer Banks* by Charles Harry Whedbee, tells a story that's ostensibly set off the North Carolina coast but is surprisingly similar to Ocean-Born Mary's in many details. The tale told in a chapter entitled "Sea-Born Woman" takes place on an Irish ship called the *Celestial Star*, on its way to New England in September 1720.

A woman named Mary O'Hagan gives birth to a baby girl as pirates are ransacking the ship. A pirate captain, Francis Spriggs, lets the passengers go free on the condition that the child is named "Jerushia Spriggs O'Hagan."

There are many more parallels; it appears that someone lifted Ocean-Born Mary from New Hampshire and plunked her down on the Outer Banks, as if the region didn't have enough legends of its own. The North Carolina version of the story is also woven into a 2002 mystery novel, *Sea-Born Women*, by B.J. Mountford.

As discussed at length later in this book, many other articles and books on New England legends and ghost stories—in particular the books of Hans Holzer in the 1960s—promoted questionable versions of the Ocean-Born Mary story to wide audiences.

THE OCEAN-BORN MARY HOUSES

A dark and stately eighteenth-century mansion by the side of a hilly road in the outskirts of Henniker is widely known as the Ocean-Born Mary House. It can be said with certainty, however, that Mary never actually lived there. The reasons for the widespread misconception will be explored shortly.

A house in which Mary is said to have lived as a girl stood beside Auburn Road in Londonderry, in an area known as Wilson's Crossing. According to *Willey's Book of Nutfield* by George F. Willey, published in 1895, the house was built "prior to 1730" by James Wilson. Other sources put the time of the house's construction at about 1690, but that seems highly unlikely—there was no settlement at Londonderry at that time.

The James Wilson who built the house was, obviously, not Mary's father. That James Wilson had died soon after the family's arrival in Boston in 1720. The relationship between Mary's father and the man who built the house is hard to figure, as there were several James Wilsons in Londonderry about that time. (Two of them were known as "Black Jim" and "Curly Jim," differentiated by their hair.)

According to Robert C. Mack's 1869 book, *The Londonderry Celebration: Exercises on the 150th Anniversary of the Settlement of Old Nutfield*, the James Wilson who settled at Wilson's Crossing arrived in Londonderry "about 1728." In any case, the house was long known as the Old Wilson House. At least five generations of the Wilsons had been born in the house.

The Old Wilson House in Londonderry before its move to Rhode Island. From *Willey's Book of Nutfield.*

James Garvin, architectural historian for the State of New Hampshire, believes that some of the carpentry details of the house are similar to the circa 1725 Reverend William Morrison House in Londonderry. The gambrel roof and the high ceilings of the Old Wilson House seem somewhat unusual, however; the other known houses in Londonderry in the same period had saltbox or gable roofs.

The house was built from lumber that grew on the grounds. It was supported by timbers two feet square. "The chimney," Willey wrote, "was built on a foundation of stone twelve feet square, and made with three fireplaces, one of which was large enough for a log six feet long."

The Old Wilson House was dismantled and moved away from Londonderry in 1937. The owner of the house at the time, the avid preservationist Carlton Richmond, relocated each numbered piece to Little Compton, Rhode Island. The reassembled house was given new shingles, a modern kitchen and baths. The interior remodeling and installation of heat and air conditioning was done in a subtle way so that the house retains its eighteenth-century appearance. The house was furnished with antiques appropriate to its period.

The Little Compton Historical Society was founded in the same year the house was moved to the town. Carlton C. Brownell of the society called the

The Truth Behind a New Hampshire Legend

The Seabourne Mary House in Little Compton, Rhode Island. *Photo by Jeremy D'Entremont.*

original restoration of the house "museum quality." Little Compton's gain was a sad event for lovers of Londonderry's history. The house move is said to have led to the founding of the Londonderry Historical Society in 1956, as residents wanted to prevent any more history from leaving the town.

Dick and Anne Keigher, who split their time between Little Compton and a 1754 house in Charleston, South Carolina, now own the Seabourne Mary House, as it's known in Rhode Island. The beautifully maintained historic home is opened for occasional public tours.

Anne Keigher is a conservation architect who has received much praise for her restoration of the London house in which Benjamin Franklin lived for sixteen years. The goal of the Keighers has been to conserve the Seabourne Mary House and to expand the living spaces by utilizing eighteenth-century post-and-beam construction techniques and antique materials where possible. It's difficult for the average visitor to differentiate a relatively recent addition to the house from the original structure.

Beginning in May 1722, when Mary's mother married James Clark, the family probably lived on the Londonderry farm that remained in the Clark family through at least two subsequent generations. Consequently, it seems

Interior of the Seabourne
Mary House in Little
Compton, Rhode Island.
Photo by Jeremy D'Entremont.

likely that Mary lived in the Seabourne Mary House for no more than a
brief period in her early childhood. As with so many aspects of the Ocean-
Born Mary story, it's difficult to be certain of all the details.

During Mary's married life with James Wallace (1742–1791), it's likely
that they lived in a farmhouse on Wallace's property in Londonderry. That
house is almost certainly no longer standing.

In her last years (1798–1814), Mary Wallace lived in Henniker with her
son William, as previously noted. William Wallace's house no longer stands,
having burned down in the early 1920s. For some years the house had been
used as Henniker's "poor farm." The foundation of the house can still
be seen on private property a little over a mile from Mary's son Robert's
prominent house on Bear Hill Road.

The Truth Behind a New Hampshire Legend

A rare photo of the William Wallace house, which burned down in the early 1920s.

The truth was later blurred to the point that it became widely believed that Mary lived her last years in her son Robert's house. This notion dates back at least to the late 1800s. An article published in a number of newspapers in 1899 included a drawing of Robert Wallace's house with the caption, "House where Ocean Mary died." Elsewhere in the article it was stated that Mary lived for many years in the house. Picture postcards from the early 1900s also called the house the "Ocean Mary House."

Over the years, many writers have repeated the misinformation that Mary lived in Robert's house. In his booklet *New England's Ghostly Haunts*, Robert Ellis Cahill goes so far as to state that Mary had many interesting guests at the house, a list that included, he claimed, Daniel Webster, Franklin Pierce and General Lafayette.

Any evidence that these people visited the house seems to be nonexistent. Pierce, a New Hampshire resident, may have visited, but the future president was only nine years old when Mary died. It seems more likely that Webster, another New Hampshire native, may have visited Robert Wallace at the house; they were both lawyers with an interest in politics.

Gussie Roy, the house's owner beginning in 1917, always insisted that it was built by the pirate captain of the Ocean-Born Mary story. There is not one shred of evidence to support this, aside from Roy's claims. In fact, there's much hard evidence to the contrary.

According to a 1904 article in the *Henniker Courier* by Leander W. Cogswell, Robert Wallace's home was so prominent that the area around it was known as the "Wallace Highlands." The house contained four large rooms on the first floor and four bedrooms and two smaller rooms on the second floor.

The hearth inside the Robert Wallace house, from the Historic American Buildings Survey in 1965, Gerda Peterich, photographer. *Courtesy of the Library of Congress, Prints and Photographs Division, Historic American Buildings Survey, reproduction number NH-160-6.*

There were six fireplaces. A 1973 real estate ad cited the huge kitchen fireplace; with its eight-foot, six-inch opening and a twelve-pie oven, it was said to be one of the largest fireplaces in New Hampshire.

In his 1935 work *Ocean-Born Mary: A Romance*, Gussie Roy showed his knowledge of architecture and antiques in his mostly accurate description of the house:

> *Large, four-square high-posted, with hipped roof, and painted red with white trimmings and green doors. The large mansion with its ells and three great barns was framed with massive timbers and fastened with oak pins. It had four entrances. One at each side. The massive doors being hung on long strap hinges, each running the full width of the door. The hinges on the front door, however, were of the crane type, it being much larger and heavier than the rest. All the doors had the "Double-Cross Witch-doors" as they were called, as it was thought that these crosses would keep the witches from entering.*

The Truth Behind a New Hampshire Legend

The white and blue room, paneled in wood, on its north side, had deep cornices and blue panels painted on its plastered walls; each with a buff stripe and with blue stenciled border at the top.

The large twenty-four light windows had real glass brought from the coast...

The staircase in the front hall, perhaps the finest piece of workmanship about the mansion, had delicately turned spindles and a very high rail... This lovely staircase was enclosed in fine paneling and was much admired by all who saw it.

Primeval pines furnished long wide boards for the wainscoting and paneling.

Stairs inside the Robert Wallace house, from the Historic American Buildings Survey in 1965, Gerda Peterich, photographer. *Courtesy of the Library of Congress, Prints and Photographs Division, Historic American Buildings Survey, reproduction number NH-160-3.*

Inside shutters, those sliding into the wall, were placed on all the windows of the first floor...

All the floors were laid as were ships decks, and in the kitchen with its massive fire-place and brick oven, the floor was slanted like a ships deck from the great hearth-stone to the outer wall. Also were the door and window frames slanted...

Francis L. Childs, a longtime professor of English at Dartmouth College, was an expert on Henniker history and Ocean-Born Mary, and he believed that the house was built between 1784 and 1786. That matches a 1904

This historic marker stands in front of the Robert Wallace home in Henniker. *Photo by Jeremy D'Entremont.*

article by Leander W. Cogswell, who wrote that the "noble old mansion" was built "shortly after the close of the Revolutionary War."

The architect of the house is unknown; according to the Historic American Buildings Survey, it might have been Robert Wallace himself. According to the survey, "The highly academic and imposing quality of the overall form, roof, and elevation of the house is very unusual in this rural locality; it most closely resembles the sophisticated pre-Revolutionary houses of Portsmouth."

David Russell, a former owner of the house, believed that it was built for a sea captain. He based his assertion on the hand-wrought wood paneling in the interior, typical of the work of ship's carpenters, and also on the gently curved kitchen floor, which he said was meant to suggest the floor inside a ship.

It's easy to understand Russell's view, but it doesn't take much of a stretch of the imagination to think that Robert Wallace, a very successful and wealthy man (although not a sea captain), might have had a house built that was similar to the sea captain's homes of the period.

In his *Architectural Heritage of the Merrimack*, John Mead Howells pointed out that Robert Wallace undoubtedly would have done business in Portsmouth on the New Hampshire seacoast and that he had probably been impressed by some of the homes he saw there. Wallace's house closely resembles the 1725 Henry Sherburne House on Deer Street in Portsmouth, now used for offices.

After Robert Wallace died in January 1815, his son, Robert Jr. (owner of a saw- and gristmill in West Henniker), rented the house for a time to various tenants. It was sold in 1834 to the farmer Washington Berry, who owned it for thirty years. Harris Campbell purchased it in 1864. A few years later, James Dowlin acquired the property.

The house had deteriorated badly and had been vacant for some years by the time it was purchased by L.M.A. "Gussie" Roy, the central character in its heyday as a celebrated "haunted house." Roy sold the house in the early 1960s to David and Corinne Russell.

When the Russells decided to sell the house in the early 1970s, the asking price was $100,000, including 130 acres of land. Bob and Mary Gregg bought the house in 1973. A 1996 article in *Yankee* praised their restoration work: "All in all, there's not a single square foot that 'needs work.' It's all absolutely gorgeous." The Greggs removed a pair of dormer windows that were not original to the house.

The present owners, Bob and Terry Stamps, purchased the property in 2000. They are active in Henniker town affairs, and they have lovingly continued the never-ending restoration of the Robert Wallace mansion.

GUSSIE ROY AND THE SELLING OF THE LEGEND

Louis Maurice Auguste Roy, the man who made the house Robert Wallace built in Henniker world famous, was an artist, photographer, antiquarian and expert on colonial handcrafts. He was also, as a friend once said of him, "a small man in stature who had big ideas."

Roy was, on a smaller scale, the P.T. Barnum of New Hampshire. Echoing the statement often attributed to Barnum about a sucker being born every minute, Roy was known to tell friends, "Nobody knows a millionth thing about anything," adding, "Sometimes I think I think too much." An eager and gullible press, hungry for a good story that would sell newspapers, was perfectly willing to promote Roy's tall tales as fact.

Born on June 23, 1883, and known to most as "Gussie," Roy was the son of a physician in St. Paul, Minnesota, also named Louis Maurice Auguste Roy. The elder L.M.A. Roy died in 1886 of diphtheria at the age of thirty-eight. Gussie's six-year-old sister had died a week earlier of the same disease. His mother, Flora E. (Quinn) Roy, was a native of Farmington, Maine. One of her close childhood friends there had been the renowned soprano Lillian Nordica.

By the early 1900s, Gussie Roy and his mother were living in La Crosse, Wisconsin. The 1903 town directory listed Roy as a "physical director" at the YMCA, and he was also one of the editors of a monthly YMCA publication. In 1905, Roy was working as an operator at an engraving company in La Crosse. By 1910, he was working as a photographer. He became a member

Gussie Roy, from the
Yankee magazine archive,
Blackington Collection.
*Courtesy of the Henniker
Historical Society.*

of the Pictorial Photographers of America and won three medals for his work in 1913 alone.

A 1978 thesis paper by Edwin L. Hill concerning photography in La Crosse had the following to say about Gussie Roy and his work:

> *"Gussie" Roy is remembered with respect and friendliness by many local residents, and he seems to be regarded as a better or more creative artist than other photographers of his time. He made his own greeting cards for a number of years. These were photographic studies mounted on card stock, with such titles as "old memories," "the night before Christmas," and similar themes. The elderly woman used as a model in some of these studies was Roy's mother.*
>
> *"Gussie" Roy portraits from the decade 1910 to 1920 exhibit a rather artistic if not sentimental approach to photography, and still carry a prestigious air. Some are signed. Roy was a photographer for special occasions and particular people.*

Roy had moderate success as a professional photographer, and some of his awards are now on display at the Henniker Historical Society. His photographic work—mostly black-and-white—was exhibited over the years at the New Hampshire State Library, the Currier Museum of Art, the Metropolitan Museum of Art and the National Gallery of Art in Washington, D.C. One of his color photos was used as the cover of *Ansco* magazine in the late 1950s.

In the 1930s, Roy was hired for a federal art project under the Works Progress Administration. Some of his photographs of antiques and traditional craftspeople produced for this project are in the collection of the University of New Hampshire.

Articles written by Roy for photographic publications included such technical titles as "Homemade Photographic Scales," "A Shade for a Twin-

Photo by Gussie Roy of his mother, Flora Roy, titled "The Night Before Christmas." *Courtesy of Phillip Seven Esser.*

Lens Reflex" and "A Portable Reflector." Late in his life, he was still using an 1880 Rochester Optical Company camera.

Roy's articles on antiques and crafts, such as "Old-Time Methods of Dyeing" and "Reseating Chairs with Splints," were published in *Antiques* and *Mechanics Illustrated*, among other publications. He published a book on the colonial craft of candle making, *The Candle Book*, in 1938.

The Roy family, according to a newspaper article, had once been rich, but they had lost their wealth through unwise investments. In 1916, Roy contacted the Henniker postmaster, who also dabbled in real estate, wondering if there were any interesting old places for sale in the area in which he could live with his widowed mother. The postmaster was about to throw the letter in the trash when a woman working in the postmaster's office, Marion Connor, asked if she could answer it. She wrote back to Roy and told him about the old Robert Wallace place.

Roy later claimed that he felt the spirit of Ocean-Born Mary reaching out to him and selecting him as the one she wanted to restore "her" house. Within two weeks, Roy had bought the magnificent house that had been built for Mary's son, Robert Wallace, in the 1780s. According to press reports, the house, which had been vacant for some years, was purchased along with one hundred acres of land through a "New York farm agency."

Gussie Roy soon moved with his mother from Wisconsin to New Hampshire. He set about restoring the old mansion and filling it with period furniture and antiques. After a while, he started telling people that Ocean-Born Mary had lived in the house and that the furniture had been hers.

As stated earlier, Mary Wallace lived her last years in Henniker with her son William, not in the house built for her son Robert and eventually bought by Gussie Roy. The mistaken notion that the Robert Wallace house was where Ocean-Born Mary had lived didn't originate with Gussie Roy; the idea dates back at least to the late 1800s. But Roy seized the idea and ran with it. He would expand the legends associated with Mary and the house to incredible proportions over the next several decades.

Roy had gotten his publicity machine in gear by the mid-1920s. The *Boston Post* featured the Ocean-Born Mary story and Roy's house in a four-page spread in September 1925. Then, on April 29, 1927, the Associated Press distributed a story with the headline, "Ghostly Stage Drives Up to Haunted Place."

The Truth Behind a New Hampshire Legend

According to the article, a "ghostly stage" was often seen approaching the so-called Ocean-Born Mary House, with a "flimsy figure" that would get off the coach, look into a well near the house and then disappear again with the coach. The ghostly figure was thought by some to be "Ocean Mary, seeking something she lost in the well." Others claimed, according to the article, that "a body was once thrust into the hole after a murder" and that "a guilty conscience brings the murderess back to the scene of the crime."

The article reported that Flora Roy "smilingly" admitted that "doors sometimes open mysteriously in the night, but she likes the mansion despite its reputed 'ghostly' visitors."

By the late 1920s, the Roys had firmly established in the collective mind of the press the idea that the house they owned was, indeed, the one in which Mary Wallace had lived. Gussie Roy also began to promote the notion that the pirate captain of the Ocean-Born Mary story had built the house after he retired from the sea and that he had buried treasure somewhere in or nearby the house.

Gussie and Flora Roy were probably making small amounts of money for providing tours of the house by the late 1920s. When the Depression hit, the flow of visitors undoubtedly decreased. To keep the tourists coming, Gussie had to invent taller and taller tales.

Gussie Roy often told the press that he hoped that a movie about Ocean-Born Mary would be made at his home. In May 1930, the *Nashua Telegraph* announced that the house would be "the scene of a movie world this summer." No such production ever happened. Later, another newspaper reported that offers had been received from motion picture companies but that Roy wanted to "wait a little while and see what happens."

It was the promotion of the house as the location of hidden pirate treasure that brought curiosity seekers in greater numbers. Eventually, Roy started renting shovels for fifty cents so that visitors could dig for gold in his orchard.

An article in the *Telegraph* in August 1930 reported that a "real treasure hunt" had started at the house. A "big pile of rocks" in the "dungeon-like" cellar, which the owners had decided "was put there for a reason," was to be removed. It would take several days or a week to remove the rocks, the article noted.

A full-page, illustrated article appeared in many newspapers nationwide in the fall of 1930, with the title, "Hunting Pirate Treasure in New England's

'Mystery House.'" The article included some new twists on the traditional Ocean-Born Mary story, and it declared the house in Henniker to be "more than a little like the Gateway to the Unknown."

The infant Mary, according to the article, was three days old when pirates boarded the immigrant ship. The pirate captain, the writer claimed, held the baby aloft in "one big, hairy hand" and sprinkled her with salt water from a bucket. "In the name of my sainted mother," he bellowed, according to the writer, "I christen thee Ocean-Born Mary. Live, child, and may you prosper."

The Roys had nothing to sell and were not inclined toward sensationalism, the writer claimed, but Roy was "not the kind of man to be stumped by an ordinary mystery." If there was something he didn't know about the house, he told the writer that he intended to find out about it.

The Roys were heavily promoting the house as haunted by this time, and their efforts were bearing fruit. The article described the once deserted road leading to the house as "lined with parked automobiles," with visitors sitting by the roadside in fascination.

The article noted that soon after they had moved into the house, Gussie Roy was awakened late one snowy night by the sound of someone rattling the latch on the front door. When he went downstairs, the door flew open and slammed shut. This was followed by a commotion as the unseen visitor noisily rushed from one dark room to another.

On Valentine's Day in 1927, the Roys were again awakened, they claimed, by someone entering the front door. According to the article, Gussie Roy "leaped down the broad staircase, revolver and flashlight in hand" in time to see the kitchen door slowly closing. Baking tins, chairs, dishes and a teakettle were strewn on the kitchen floor, Roy claimed.

Newspaper articles of this period show the further development of the "phantom stagecoach" stories associated with the house. A woman in white was frequently seen, it was claimed, running from the coach to an old well near the house. The phantom coach became a primary component of the Ocean-Born Mary story as it's appeared in scores of more recent publications.

Stories of phantom coaches have been common for centuries, especially in Irish folklore. Another possible inspiration for these stories was a description written by Leander W. Cogswell of Robert Wallace's late 1700s mode of transportation:

Judge Robert Wallace soon appeared, with a coach drawn by two horses. This carriage proved to be very convenient, for in it the judge's large family were conveyed to and from church, and it was often used upon other occasions. Chaises became quite common, and at one time almost every well-to-do farmer had his chaise. One is now rarely seen.

The extensive 1930 article provided more detail on the "real treasure hunt" mentioned previously in the *Nashua Telegraph*. Roy had discovered a pile of "curiously shaped stones" in a "secret passageway" behind a cellar wall. Roy said that he believed the passageway led to the old well outside. It would be months before excavations were completed, but "divining rod experts" were nearly certain that treasure would be found.

The fame of Gussie Roy's house continued to spread. A brief news story in August 1931 stated that the house was attracting people from all parts of the country, including the vaudeville comedian Jefferson DeAngelis and his wife.

Early in the following May, another brief story in the *Nashua Telegraph* announced that the house was again open to visitors. A long string of cars was already seen arriving at the mansion, full of tourists anxious to tour its twenty rooms.

Heavy tourist traffic continued to flow to the house in Henniker, especially on summer weekends. On Sunday, July 5, 1930, more than one hundred people signed the guest register. Flora Roy enthralled the visitors with the stories of her sightings of the ghost of Ocean-Born Mary and the phantom coach. For once, the author of the article injected a note of skepticism, adding, "or at least that is the story she tells those who come here." By this time, the *Telegraph* reported, the grounds around the house had been dug up "for miles" by Roy and other treasure seekers, to no avail.

Another widely published newspaper article in December 1934 claimed that the Roys had found a rusty tin box in the attic of their house "that had somehow been overlooked during previous inspections" and that the mysterious box contained "decayed papers that mentioned hidden wealth—jewels, doubloons, and pieces of eight." The Roys, once skeptical of the existence of ghosts, according to the writer, now believed that Ocean-Born Mary herself was trying to direct them to pirate treasure.

The 1934 article took the ghost stories to outlandish new heights. One morning, after a rainstorm, the Roys had found three bloody boot prints on the front porch that "seemed to have been made by an antiquated sea boot." Another time, they heard a voice shouting, "Any eggs today?" from the yard, and when they went outside they found "three goats, staring into the air." (It isn't clear if the goats were real or ghostly goats.)

The December 1934 article also marks an early appearance of an element that became a staple of the Ocean-Born Mary tale: the idea that the pirate captain had built the Henniker mansion when he had "tired of scuttling ships and slashing throats."

The writer stated that the pirate then invited Mary and her husband and sons to the mansion to live, on the condition that he would be allowed to occupy a "special room" he had built for himself. Soon after Mary and her family moved in, the pirate captain was attacked and killed by one of his old crew, apparently trying to find where their treasure had been hidden.

In a 1935 letter, Roy wrote, "The architects say that this floor, etc., is proof that the house was built by a sea captain, and that a farmer would not have any slanting floors like a ship's deck to remind him of the sea. So I think that proves that the builder was a sea captain and a pirate perhaps."

This was wishful thinking on Roy's part. The idea that the pirate captain had the house built and that Mary went to live there is clearly wrong. Records show that Mary didn't move from Londonderry to Henniker until 1798. Assuming the pirate to be at least twenty-five when he attacked Mary's ship in 1720, he would have to have been over one hundred years old in 1798. In addition, it's abundantly clear that the house was built for Robert Wallace and not for a pirate or sea captain.

By the mid-1930s, Roy had built a "special detecting machine" to search for pirate treasure, with earphones and "detector tubes." In spite of the newfangled equipment, it was reported that he had found only a few nails, horseshoes and rusty hinges.

By the summer of 1935, Wallace Mack, a descendant of Mary Wallace, had presented to the Roys a piece of silk cut from Mary's wedding dress. The silk was framed and put on display for visitors to see. It was reported that in July 1935, on the anniversary of Mary's birth, mediums "were sure" that the spirit of Ocean-Born Mary would make an appearance because of the return of the silk to the house.

Despite the presence of reporters from more than a dozen newspapers and mediums who "went into deep trances," nothing stirred but the wind. Some unnamed persons, however, according to the *Telegraph*, "sensed the presence of a big black bearded pirate" who brought the message that treasure was buried on the property.

By this time, Gussie Roy had discovered an American eagle painted over one of the fireplaces in the house. The eagle held an olive branch in its talons, and above its head there were sixteen stars. In later years, Roy insisted that Mary Wallace herself had painted the eagle, although there was no evidence to back up the idea.

Researcher Andrew Rothovius, who wrote articles on Ocean-Born Mary in the 1960s, believed that the eagle was most likely painted by "one of the itinerant early nineteenth century painters who were the forerunners of today's interior decorators." In any case, the eagle was lovingly restored by Gussie Roy.

For many years, Flora Roy often served as a tour guide for visitors to the house. The writer of a 1935 article described her "delightful manner" and

This American eagle painted over a fireplace in the Robert Wallace house was discovered and restored by Gussie Roy. *Photo by Jeremy D'Entremont.*

Photo by Gussie
Roy of his mother
inside their home
in Henniker, circa
1936. *Courtesy of
Phillip Seven Esser.*

said that after one of Mrs. Roy's tours, "even the more skeptical feel that after all strange things do happen in this world of ours and certainly she has a right to her own belief regardless."

In many ways, Ocean-Born Mary mania peaked in 1935. That year, Gussie Roy wrote his opus on the subject: *Ocean-Born Mary: A Romance.* You can find a copy of Roy's typescript at the Henniker Historical Society.

In his odd twenty-one-page work, Roy fleshes out the Ocean-Born Mary tale with a detailed and fanciful backstory that takes place in Ireland. The primary characters are a young woman named "Jane Rawson," daughter of a weaver, "James Allyne," son of a blacksmith, and "Henry Cunningham, son of Sir Charles, who lived in the old mansion on the hill."

The Truth Behind a New Hampshire Legend

In Roy's story, Henry's love for Jane is forbidden by his father, Sir Charles, who doesn't want his son marrying a poor weaver's daughter. Sir Charles invents a mission for his son, who is forced to leave for France. Meanwhile, Jane, encouraged by Sir Charles, marries James Allyne. Henry returns from France a short time later and is devastated to discover that his true love has married another. The jilted Henry takes to the sea and becomes a pirate captain, using the pseudonym "Captain Pedro."

Roy's story seems to mark the first appearance of "Pedro" as the pirate's name. On his first page, Roy stated that the names in the story were fictitious. Just the same, the name "Captain Pedro" or "Don Pedro" became a standard part of the Ocean-Born Mary story.

For a while, Roy's version more or less converges with the Ocean-Born Mary story as it was commonly told. Jane and James sail to "the promised land" in 1720 aboard the ship *Hope*. A few days after the birth of Jane's daughter, a crew of pirates led by Captain Pedro boards the ship.

In his pirate garb, and with his skin darkened with the juice of walnuts, the pirate is unrecognizable to Jane as her former love. She allows him to name the infant Mary in exchange for the lives of the passengers.

Here Roy's version diverges again from the traditional story. The pirate of Roy's version is eventually pardoned by the king and is awarded a land grant on the banks of the Contoocook, where he builds a mansion. After Mary's husband dies, she goes to live in the pirate's mansion with her young children.

Mary then witnesses the pirate burying his treasure on the grounds of the house. Some years later, just after he sees the traditional sailor's warning of the *Flying Dutchman* ghost ship in the setting sun, Pedro is murdered by a rival pirate. His body is buried beneath the hearthstone in the kitchen.

Roy's writing is dry but occasionally dramatic, such as his description of the moment when Henry learns of Jane's marriage to James:

> *Then Henry flung his glass of liquor high above his head, flung it to the floor with a crash crying, "To hell with Sir Charles and the King too." With that, he strode to the door, and with high-pitched laughter that froze the marrow of ones' bones, disappeared into the dusk. The villagers stood like statues as they heard the sound of galloping hoofs in the distance.*

And then there is the moment when the pirate sees the newborn baby girl: "So he leaned over the berth, and putting his large rough hand on the tiny head, softly pronounced one word, 'Mary,' and a large tear dropped from the Captain's eye to the coverlet."

Near the end of *Ocean-Born Mary: A Romance*, Roy describes an "old negro" slave's sighting of a ghostly white coach carrying Mary and Captain Pedro. Roy concludes, "[I]t is said that they [Mary and Pedro] will always remain near the old mansion which they loved so well."

The pirate's treasure had yet to be found, but Roy added a final note: "If the propesy [*sic*] is fulfilled and the treasure is found, a sequel will be written, telling the details of its finding and disposal."

An article that appeared in the *Telegraph* in January 1936, accompanied by Gussie Roy's photograph of his mother in period garb writing at a two-hundred-year-old desk in their house, was notable for dragging Captain Kidd into the Ocean-Born Mary story. The writer stated that there were "at least two families" in Henniker who scoffed at the idea of pirate treasure on the property. But, the writer claimed, the infamous Captain Kidd had, in fact, "wandered as far as Robb's Pond in the neighboring town of Antrim, bringing with him much fine gold." In actual fact, a pirate treasure furor had been started in Antrim in 1823 as a practical joke. It's unlikely that Kidd was ever anywhere in the vicinity.

The writer of the 1936 article postulated that the ghost of the pirate captain might be haunting the place because he was "still looking for the woman whom he knew as a tiny babe in a little cabin on board a ship many years ago." The ghost stories may have been "bunk" to many people in Henniker, according to the writer, but "strange things actually do happen here."

Much of the writing of Carl Carmer (1893–1976), a popular author, focused on American myths and folklore. He included a chapter on Ocean-Born Mary in his 1937 book, *The Hurricane's Children*.

Carmer's book presented the Roy version of the story as fact and heavily promoted the ghost angle. "Some curious folks who went there at twilight," he wrote, "claimed that they saw a very tall woman of great beauty walking down the high-railinged stair." He added detail to the usual phantom coach story, claiming that immediately after the coach was typically seen, there came "from the old orchard back of the house, fearful groans as of a man in mortal pain."

The Truth Behind a New Hampshire Legend

When he visited the house, Carmer asked Flora Roy why she didn't have the hearthstone lifted to see if the bones of the pirate captain were buried there. She replied that it would cost $150 to have that done, and with that money she could buy a lot of things more useful to her than a skeleton.

The pirate treasure subplot took a startling new twist in the summer of 1937, when it was announced in the *Telegraph* that a "medium from Lawrence, Mass." had "pointed out the exact spot where a brass-bound chest is hidden." Gussie Roy planned to start digging as soon as he could "interest enough vacationists to assist in the work." According to the medium, the newspaper claimed, the "rather small chest" was buried several feet underground, near a small brook about a hundred yards from the house.

In early October 1937, a crowd gathered in breathless anticipation at the Roys' property as Dana Brown walked around the grounds with a divining rod. Brown, the *Telegraph* reported, had recently found "Frank Gay's gold watch buried in eight inches of mud" and, as a result, had been getting requests to search for all kinds of things.

Brown wandered the yard for six hours that day, pausing whenever his witch-hazel rod pointed downward. Every time this happened, several men dug into the moist earth with shovels. More nails, a horseshoe, an iron kettle and pieces of scrap iron were all that was found.

Treasure fever persisted despite the lack of results. Roy's claims were sometimes very specific about the treasure, as in one widely published article that claimed the pirate had buried $7 million worth of gold bars before he was found with "a cutlass through his throat."

With the expanse of land around the house, there were always more places to dig. Some years later, it was reported that "some psychics in Portland, Maine" told Roy that the pirate's treasure was buried "near an old tree." Much digging ensued around a very old tree near the house, with no results. Roy asked the Portland psychics for more detail, and the word came back: "She says it is not near the tree you think."

A large feature on Ocean-Born Mary, written by Eleanor Roberts, appeared in the *Boston Sunday Post* on October 2, 1938. Roberts described the experience of a "Concord, New Hampshire, policeman" who, with a friend, was said to have witnessed "a gray-ghost of a coach with four big horses" draw up to the house, with a "tall, white clad woman" pulling the reins. An article in the 1960s repeated the *Post* story and named the policeman as "Scott Rogers."

Marion Lowndes's 1941 book *Ghosts that Still Walk* expanded the policeman story, claiming that a Concord policeman and some of his friends saw the apparition. In Lowndes's version, however, the men didn't see the coach; instead, they saw "[a] woman in white, a tall woman…walking with a firm unhurried step toward the well under the old apple tree at the side of the house."

Roberts's 1938 article added much fuel to the fire of Roy's tales. The author described her visit to the house and her encounter with the eighty-year-old Flora Roy with much colorful detail:

> *It was a gray, murky day that we drove up to the lonesome house in the New Hampshire countryside, with the weeds running ragged over the stone steps, and the trees sighing sadly in the wind.*
>
> *There was that pregnant silence about the place that makes you feel that something was about to happen. The knock that resounded on the door marked with the crusader's cross to ward off evil spirits, crashed into the stillness.*
>
> *And finally the door opened. Swung back as though on oiled hinges! There stood the tiniest, shrunken old lady from another world entirely. In her long green velvet dress with its fine lace collar she looked as though she was still living in the last century. Her white hair was like feathers of faint rain against her face.*
>
> *Was this the reincarnation of the woman who died more than 120 years ago? Her gnarled old hands trembled against the yellow-gray wood of the door. In a quavering voice she beckoned us to come in.*
>
> *Come in—to the room where Ocean-Born Mary lay in her coffin—to the room where everyone died. Perhaps to the room where a fortune in gold lay buried.*

"My son and I have spent many long, lonely years searching for that pirate's gold," Flora Roy told Roberts. "And mark my words, we will find it. It is here. There is no doubt of it. We are just waiting for Mary to tell us when she wants us to take it."

Roberts was drawn in by Flora Roy's apparent sincerity, as were, no doubt, many of her readers. "Looking into those mild, blue eyes," she wrote, "that trusting, hopeful smile, and the hands that fluttered over her lap like sad, hurt sparrows, it was hard to disbelieve such faith."

Flora E. Roy, photo by
L.M.A. (Gussie) Roy.
*Courtesy of the Henniker
Historical Society.*

Flora and Gussie Roy told Roberts that there was a particular room on the first floor where the sick were taken in days past, because of its convenient location and because the room received the most sunlight. "It is in this room that all the queer manifestations take place, rappings, noises, whispering voices," Roberts wrote.

Flora Roy claimed that she coughed more in that room than anywhere else in the house, and Gussie was quick to offer an explanation: "Someone in this room died of tuberculosis. When Mother sits in this room at the old spinning wheel, or playing the organ, her whole body is wracked by terrible spells of choking."

Gussie Roy had a knack for connecting real features of the house to his tall tales, seemingly lending them authenticity. He told Roberts about a hidden back stairway he had found, all boarded up. When he explored the narrow old stairs, he had a "roily feeling in the pit of his stomach," which he attributed to some tragic event in the past. "Perhaps Ocean-Born Mary was killed by a fall on those stairs, and ever afterwards they were boarded up," he said.

Ocean-Born Mary, on occasion, made her way into some of the more prestigious national media. No less a publication than *National Geographic* published an account in April 1939. It was included as part of the magazine's coverage of the hurricane that had swept New England in September 1938, killing more than seven hundred people and downing many thousands of trees. A photo by Gussie Roy of his house, with his mother in the doorway, is accompanied by this caption:

> *The lady who lives here says she saw a tall woman, with skirts whipping wildly, watching her son while he tried to prop his garage during the hurricane. Later the large elm tree at the right fell without touching the house. They believe the mysterious visitor was the ghost of "Ocean-Born Mary," who lived here long ago, and that she protected her home and its inhabitants from harm.*

The idea that Mary's ghost or other mysterious forces protected Gussie Roy and his house was a recurring theme. Another article presented the hurricane story with additional detail:

> *Trees began to fall as winds reached ferocious heights. The long walk to the front door was strewn with ripped branches, but he made it safely to the house, His mother, watching from the door, claimed she saw Mary hovering over him—her arms outstretched defending him.*

A 1951 article described another incident when the Roys claimed Mary's ghost saved the day. Gussie Roy and his mother were burning trash from the house one day when his mother found a tied-up paper bag. "What do you suppose is in it?" she asked her son. She immediately answered her own question, "Nothing of interest, I guess." As she started to throw the bag into the fire, Gussie stopped her in the nick of time.

"What do you suppose was in it?" Roy said. "Two pounds of blasting powder! Now how do you account for that?"

The Truth Behind a New Hampshire Legend

In 1981, the *Weekly World News* included this incident in a dubious story with the title, "Ghosts to the Rescue." The writer twisted the story so that it was almost unrecognizable:

> *When Angus* [sic] *Roy bought an ancient house in Henniker, NH, he scoffed at tales that the house was haunted by someone known locally as "Ocean Born Mary." But cleaning up the place, he was about to throw an old paper bag in the fire when his wrist was suddenly gripped by an icy hand.*
>
> *Recovering from his panic, he found no one at all in the house—but the paper bag held several pounds of blasting powder.*

In 1946, the popular New England historian and author Edward Rowe Snow visited Roy. Snow described the visit in his books *Legends of the New England Coast* and *Supernatural Mysteries and Other Tales*. At the time, Roy was making and selling "tiny photographs." Snow wrote that Roy regaled him with the story of how the pirate captain retired from the sea, sailed up the Contoocook River and had his home built in Henniker. Roy also told Snow that Mary had died in the "Eagle Room" on the second floor of the house.

In what may have been an extra effort to impress Snow, who was a lover of pirate lore, Roy told him that the pirate who had boarded the ship from Ireland in 1720 was Captain Kidd himself. Snow pointed out that Kidd had been hanged in 1701, making it unlikely that he was still robbing ships nineteen years later.

In *Supernatural Mysteries and Other Tales*, Snow mentioned discussions that he had in Boston with George Allan England, who claimed to have lifted (with much help, presumably) the giant hearthstone in the so-called Ocean-Born Mary House. England reported that there was absolutely nothing underneath. Others present later claimed that there was a skeleton underneath, but England said that there was nothing of the sort.

An article in the *Boston Sunday Post* on November 30, 1947, contained some of the most outlandish claims yet. Among many other distortions, the writer, Carol Auburn, claimed that the pirate of the story was Philip Babb, who had taken over as "chief cutthroat of the high seas" when Captain Kidd was hanged.

Auburn also wrote that, after Mary's death, the house in Henniker was closed, locked and left deserted for one hundred years. She told of a woman who was given a tour of the house by the ghost of Ocean-Born Mary herself, before the Roys moved in. Like so many stories on Ocean-Born Mary in so many reputable publications, this is all presented as absolute fact.

The guestbook in the house in 1952 recorded the names of 1,267 visitors from Maine to California, as well as some foreign countries. One Henniker resident commented that far more photos were taken of the Wallace house than had ever been taken of the President Franklin Pierce mansion a few miles away in Hillsborough.

In the book *Strangely Enough*, published in 1959, C.B. Colby recounted a visit to the famous house in Henniker some years earlier. "Mr. Roy has told us that he lived in the old house with his mother, and as we were looking at the stone a lady passed silently by the doorway to the outer hall," Colby wrote. "My daughter and I watched her but she did not join us or listen to her son repeat the familiar tale once more. We thought no more about it."

When the visitors were about to leave, they mentioned that they had seen Roy's mother. "My mother?" Roy exclaimed. "In the hall? Why, she hasn't been out of bed in months—she's a helpless invalid." Colby wondered, "Just who was it we saw pass the hall door as we stood by Captain Pedro's tomb under the hearth of the 'Ocean-born Mary' house on that windswept day?"

Flora Roy died in 1949. A *Parade* magazine article on April 30 of the following year promoted Roy's stories as gospel, including the one about Ocean-Born Mary's ghost saving his life in the great hurricane of 1938. Gussie told the writer that he wasn't psychic but that there was "a presence there [in the house]. Everyone feels it right away."

Marion Connor, the woman who had told Gussie Roy that the "old Wallace house" was available to buy in 1916, wrote an article that appeared in the May 1954 edition of *New Hampshire Profiles*. Connor went against the prevailing tide and did her best to separate the fact and legend of the Ocean-Born Mary story. She called Roy's pirate and ghost stories "quite a body of fanciful literature," but she gave him credit for restoring the "fine historic house."

Roy did a great deal to bring the house back to life in the early years of his ownership. In spite of his best efforts, however, it seems that he had trouble keeping the house in good repair in later years. A 1951 article described the house as "in poor repair, its exterior bleak and blackened with age."

The Truth Behind a New Hampshire Legend

The popularity of the phantom coach story continued unabated through the 1950s. On Halloween night in 1954, a group of college students painted an old wagon white, rented white horses from a farmer and dressed a young woman in a white gown. The "ghostly" coach pulled in front of Gussie Roy's house about midnight. Roy was happy to play along; he called the local newspapers and swore that he'd seen Mary and her phantom coach in his front yard.

An article in the *Boston Globe* Sunday magazine section on the day before Halloween in 1955 noted, "And maybe if you watch with believing eyes you'll see the figure of Ocean-born Mary, a red haired, green eyed Irish beauty, six feet tall, step out of the coach and disappear into the house."

Gussie Roy accumulated a collection of antique curiosities that he was always happy to show to visitors. A 1958 article in the *New Hampshire Sunday News* showed two college students examining a "cooling off board," to which the bodies of the dead were strapped to flatten them out as they cooled off. An earlier article mentioned that the other curiosities exhibited by Roy included an Indian dugout canoe and a birch-bark canoe once owned by a friend of Buffalo Bill.

The 1958 article showed Roy kneeling on the hearthstone in the kitchen, "under which the pirate and his treasure are said to be buried." The article added more fodder to the haunted house angle, mentioning "strange lights gleaming from the windows at midnight...dinner candles mysteriously blown out" and "Mary's spectre periodically trying to point out Pedro's hidden treasure, or re-enacting the episode of his death."

Over the years, a house tour with Gussie Roy became more and more like a visit to a carnival funhouse. A friend, Paul Scruton, wrote after Roy's death, "Being conducted by Roy in person through the house was an awe inspiring sort of ordeal that sent shudders up and down the spines of many visitors."

Roy was known to strategically place an old rocking chair over a loose floorboard. When he stepped on the other end of the board, he'd point and say, "Look! Mary's rocking in her favorite chair." He dragged chains on the floor during tours for added effects. When the rats in the walls acted up, Roy said that the sounds were "psychic noises" and further proof that the house was haunted.

Most tourists and press eagerly ate up Roy's stories, but there were naysayers who occasionally rained on his parade. Francis L. Childs, a professor of English for forty-five years at Dartmouth College, was a scholar on Henniker history and the story of Ocean-Born Mary. Childs told anyone who'd listen that he'd never heard any talk of ghosts or pirates associated with Robert Wallace's old house before Gussie Roy bought it.

When people challenged his stories, Roy was known to say, "I'd be a lot better off if Francis Childs wouldn't talk so much."

In his last years, Gussie Roy continued to live in the house after he had sold it to David Russell, a retired welding engineer from Chelmsford, Massachusetts, and his wife, Corinne, in 1962. For a time, the Russells allowed Roy to continue giving tours of the house for twenty-five cents.

An article called "Ghost Keeper," written by Robert P. Richmond, appeared in the March 1963 issue of *New Hampshire Profiles* magazine. Richmond described the then seventy-nine-year-old Gussie Roy as a "100-pound sprite of a man," with "bright blue eyes, engaging smile, and fringe of white hair" and "an elfin charm." Richmond felt that there was "an innate dignity to the man."

"I have the feeling she is still watching over her house," Roy told Richmond. "In the first place, how many pre-Revolutionary houses are left, way back in the hills, like this one? They've either tumbled down from neglect, or burned. Yet every time it seems this house is going to be abandoned, somebody's come along to keep it going."

Roy told Richmond that as long as he cared for the house, Mary would protect him, too. Roy said that he had experienced "thirty-five bad accidents" over the years but had survived thanks to Mary's protection.

Despite being the son of a doctor, Gussie Roy had a lifelong distrust of modern medicine. He never allowed himself to be X-rayed or injected. He told Richmond that the last time he had taken medicine from a drugstore was in 1898, when he had scarlet fever. He didn't drink alcohol, coffee, tea or milk but said that he was fond of red clover blossom tea and an occasional cup of hot cocoa with a spoonful of honey. He recommended chewing juniper berries to aid kidney function.

Roy demonstrated his good health for the *New Hampshire Profiles* photographer by doing several handstands and somersaults. He engaged in regular yoga exercises, calisthenics and sunbaths.

With the responsibility of owning the house off his shoulders, Roy said that he had several projects he was pursuing, including books on old-fashioned

Gussie Roy showing off in 1963. *Photo by Stephen T. Whitney from* New Hampshire Profiles.

vegetable dyes and weaving. A Henniker resident was quoted in Richmond's article as saying, "If he'd had the breaks, Mr. Roy would be known as a distinguished photographer, and only incidentally as a bit eccentric."

An article in the *Keene Sentinel* dwelled on Roy's eccentricities. He never took a bath, the writer claimed—at least not in water. He was fond of sitting in a bathtub filled with popcorn, his favorite snack. He took daily nude sunbaths in the backyard, even after the Russells bought the house—a habit that was disconcerting to Corinne Russell's lady friends who came to socialize.

In a poignant article published in *New Hampshire Profiles* after Roy's death, his friend Josephine Messenger recalled her first visit to Roy's house in October 1960. "His ruddy round face," she wrote, "and sharp blue eyes were fringed by silver-grey hairs that stuck out at diverse angles above his ears." He wore a "clean, faded blue shirt, tan belted pants and well worn dirty sneakers." Messenger continued:

> *He smiled warmly and invited me into the haunted house. How the huge witch door had creaked and groaned as it swung back on its rusty hinges. That day he told me that Ocean Born Mary's spirit was still living in the house. It was there, too; I felt it. There were cobwebs over everything and the paper was hanging from the walls. Dim light filtered in through the dust dirty window panes.*

At the time of Messenger's visit, Roy shared the house with the last of his mother's six cats—the twenty-one-year-old, coal-black Brother. Roy showed Messenger the famous hearthstone under which, he claimed, the pirate captain was buried. "I can tell you it's cursed," he told her, "because everyone who has tried to lift it has died a horrible death."

Roy continued the tour by pointing out the stairs he called the "Bride's Stairway." There were sixteen stairs. Roy explained, "Most girls were sixteen years of age when they married."

Next on the tour was the room Roy claimed was Mary's bedchamber. Messenger was shocked to see the imprint of what appeared to be a body on the bed; even the pillow was "hollowed in and soiled, as though a head had rested there for years."

As they left the room, Roy closed the door and said, "Ocean Born Mary never likes to have her door closed." To the horror of Ms. Messenger, the latch slowly lifted on its own, and the door opened with a click. She didn't seem to consider the possibility that the latch was faulty—or perhaps she pretended not to consider it for Roy's benefit.

Messenger visited Roy several more times in the ensuing years, and they corresponded between visits. When he was seventy-nine, he told her that he could still do all of the same acrobatic exercises he did when he was eighteen and an instructor at the YMCA in La Crosse, Wisconsin.

Roy spent his last days in a nursing home. Josephine Messenger visited him shortly before his death, and she quoted him as saying, "Life is very sad. All my treasures have been taken over by strangers. My life is a failure. Now I'll never finish all I tried to do."

The Truth Behind a New Hampshire Legend

Roy asked to be buried next to his mother in the small burial plot across the street from their house in Henniker, and he requested a white wooden cross like hers. He died in a nursing home in Greenfield, New Hampshire, on September 6, 1965. Roy had a correspondence list of more than six hundred names, but only twenty people attended his funeral.

Roy's request to have the twenty-third Psalm read at his funeral was honored, and a white wooden cross was put on his grave, next to his mother's. The cross was inscribed by his friend Josephine Messenger with the words, "He sowed, others reaped."

In the years since his death, countless writers have promoted Roy's version of Mary's story as fact. Others have worked to dismantle it in a search for the truth hidden inside. It's easy to scoff at the eccentric Gussie Roy and his tall tales, but a 1998 letter printed in the *Concord Monitor* is a reminder that Roy was no villain and that good storytelling has real value. Carol S. Bohosiewicz wrote:

> *My mother, my 6-year-old daughter and I moved to Wilton in 1961. On one October day, when we were visiting Mother, we decided to drive down Route 202. The sky was deep, deep blue with the sun shining brilliantly and the leaves whisking about in the cool fall day—a true October day.*
>
> *We literally fell into Henniker, saw the Ocean-Born Mary House with a tiny sign giving entrance prices but saying "babes in arms—nothing." We decided to investigate, but after finding a seemingly empty house, we were about to go when from the top of the hill a tiny figure came bouncing down. His high-top sneakers truly seemed to have springs in them!*
>
> *Mr. Roy was absolutely mesmerizing in telling his tale. I would describe him as a bit fey, but his enthusiasm about his subject made you feel Mary would walk in the front door anytime.*
>
> *He particularly talked to my daughter, and she obviously responded to him with rapt attention (leading to a lifelong love of American history). We never paid for the tour—I suspect he enjoyed talking to us.*
>
> *Mother and I recognized at the time that he embroidered the true story, but isn't there a place for romantic legends?*
>
> *He truly could have matched any of the storytellers we pay to see today, and I think he should not be slandered for having a marvelous imagination and the ability to present it with real panache.*

Gussie Roy outside his famous house in Henniker in 1963. *Photo by Stephen T. Whitney from New Hampshire Profiles.*

Martha C. Taylor of the Henniker Historical Society wrote that Roy, shortly before his death, confessed to a friend that he knew Mary had never really lived in his house and that she didn't haunt it. All the same, Gussie Roy, his mother and countless other people had plenty of fun with the story while it lasted.

THE HENNIKER HOUSE

Haunted or Not?

Alice V. Flanders, a stenographer for the New Hampshire legislature, wrote a well-informed paper on Ocean-Born Mary in the late 1960s. Flanders knew some of the grandchildren of James Dowlin, who had owned the Robert Wallace house many years before Roy. The grandchildren recalled visiting the house, and neither they nor their grandfather felt that the place was haunted.

The present owners of the house have said that it isn't haunted, and they should know. That would seem to close the door on any discussion of the subject.

But famous ghosts die hard, and many writers have continued to promote the idea that the Robert Wallace mansion is haunted. Some very big names in the field of paranormal investigation have written extensively about purported spirits in the house. If none of the paranormal happenings attributed to the house is real, the fact that so many people believed the stories for so long looks like a case study in the powers of suggestion and wishful thinking.

Whatever the case, these stories are a prominent thread in the Ocean-Born Mary saga as it's been related in recent decades. There seem to be no published references to the house being haunted that predate the Gussie Roy era, but it's difficult to say if he originated the idea.

In a 1962 letter in the files of the Henniker Historical Society, Mrs. Chapin Hopkins of the New Hampshire Historical Society wrote, "When Robert Wallace was thrown from his horse in front of the house in 1815, rumors went

The Robert Wallace house in Henniker. His mother, Ocean-Born Mary, never lived here. *Photo by Jeremy D'Entremont.*

around that the horse had been frightened by Mary's ghost." Hopkins didn't give a source for this information. According to her letter, after the house had passed to other owners after Robert Wallace's death and had become "a bit neglected and tumbled-down," the stories of hauntings increased.

It isn't clear if Gussie Roy invented the idea of the house being haunted after he bought it in 1916, but he certainly expanded the idea and capitalized on it. As detailed in the earlier chapter on Roy, he claimed that he and his mother experienced much ghostly activity that began soon after they purchased the house.

A dubious, widely published 1930 newspaper article—possibly the source of Mrs. Chapin's reference—stated that Robert Wallace had been in charge of a detachment of "Colonial troops" at the house at the time of his mother's death. (Why there would be colonial troops decades after the establishment of the United States is anyone's guess.)

A sentry, said the writer, told Wallace that he had seen the figure of a woman in white "hovering" near the gate at midnight. The next day, as he tried to pass through the same gate, Wallace's horse was frightened and threw its rider.

The 1930 article also reported that once, near midnight some twenty-five years earlier, three men were passing by the house when they saw a "spectral stage coach" pull up near the front door. Out stepped a woman in white, "as plain as day." The woman disappeared in the direction of an old well that, the next day, "showed signs of tampering."

One of the most persistent elements of the Ocean-Born Mary ghost stories is the phantom stagecoach purportedly seen pulling up to the front of the house. According to the 1930 article, the phantom stagecoach had been seen recently, when "reputable witnesses" watched it "rumbling over the frozen road" to the house. A lady in white was seen to disembark and go to the old well, which she closed with a bang of its heavy cover. The next day, a "score of people" saw marks left by the coach and horses in the turf, and the well had been "plainly disturbed." These stories most likely were products of Gussie Roy's vivid imagination.

In his 1968 book *Real Ghosts: Restless Spirits and Haunted Minds*, the popular paranormal writer Brad Steiger claimed, "One of the townspeople, who has witnessed the ghostly carriage, is so terrified that he cannot be persuaded to return to the house, even in the daytime."

Gussie Roy always maintained that he never saw Mary's ghost with his own eyes. His mother, however, claimed to have seen her on many occasions. Also mentioned in the 1930 article is an episode purportedly experienced by Flora Roy in August 1929, when she said she was "terrified" to see a spinning wheel, covered with dust, slowly spinning and clicking by itself for a full twenty minutes.

Another 1930 article in the *Nashua Telegraph* reported that "spiritualists and mediums" had visited the Henniker house and claimed that treasure was buried in the cellar. It's not known who those mediums were; the story was most likely the invention of Gussie Roy, who was promoting the house as haunted—and the scene of buried treasure—around that time.

A paranormal investigation of sorts took place at the house in July 1937. According to an article in the *Boston Post*, a group of "students of psychic phenomena and descendants of Ocean-Born Mary" gathered at the house as the guests of Gussie Roy, hoping to make contact with Mary on the 215th anniversary of her birth. Nothing happened because "a condition was prevalent that could not be righted," according to a medium who was present at the event.

Flora E. Roy at the
spinning wheel, photo
by L.M.A. (Gussie) Roy.
*Courtesy of the Henniker
Historical Society.*

Marion Lowndes's *Ghosts that Still Walk* reported on the findings of
some mediums who had visited the Henniker home. One claimed that
she had contacted the spirit of the pirate captain. When the pirate was
asked where his treasure was hidden, the reported answer was, "I buried
it. Let her find it."

Lowndes's book quotes the wife of another medium:

> *We were up there several times, and my husband, after hearing the story,*
> *tried to see what he could get. He was very strong in getting impressions on*
> *a material subject. He got some very strong ones there. None of them as far*
> *as we know have yet materialized, so it would not be advisable to put them*

in a printed book. They may later materialize. I don't say they won't. I know from experience that you have to give spirits their own time. You can't demand of them.

It's difficult to prove the validity of psychic experiences; skeptics will always have another explanation. If there's such a thing as true mediumship, it's hard to differentiate it from the fake variety. Even with true mediums—if you accept that there may be such a thing—much of the information produced is difficult or impossible to corroborate.

The following stories of investigators and mediums visiting the so-called Ocean-Born Mary House are part of the fabric of the ever-evolving legend. Whether the accounts have any degree of validity is up to the reader to decide.

Ed and Lorraine Warren are considered by many to be the parents of modern ghost hunting in New England. Ed (1926–2006) was a demonologist and author, and Lorraine (born 1927) is a clairvoyant and trance medium who worked on many investigations with her husband. The couple founded the New England Society for Psychic Research in 1952, and they later opened the Occult Museum in Monroe, Connecticut.

Among the Warrens' most noted investigations was the infamous (and widely debunked) "Amityville Horror" case, and the movie *The Haunting in Connecticut* was also inspired by one of their cases. Their names stir endless debate among paranormal researchers; they are as revered by some as they are scorned as frauds by others.

Ed Warren once summed up his theory of the paranormal: "If you look at a fan and it's standing still, you can see the propellers very easily. But, if that fan starts up you can't see anything—it's invisible. Spirits are on that different vibrational field. They're all around us right now, but you can't see them. But if you were like Lorraine, you could see them clairvisually, hear them clairaudioally."

According to the Warrens, it was at the so-called Ocean-Born Mary House in Henniker that Lorraine's clairvoyant powers first manifested. Ed Warren once related the following story:

I was with Lorraine and another couple that we used to socialize with. We were probably about 19 or 20 years old at the time…Anyway, we were driving through New Hampshire and I see this sign that says "Henniker." I looked back at my friend Jerry who was in the back seat and said that I had heard of a haunted house...the "Ocean Born Mary" house and that it was in Henniker.

We pulled up front, and man, I gotta tell you, it sure did look haunted from the outside...I knew if anybody could get us in, it would be Lorraine with her Irish charm and all. We watched as she knocked on the door. We saw this light in a window high above, then the light reached the lower level and finally the door opened. We could barely make it out, but soon we saw Lorraine motioning for us to come on up. To make a long story short we all got into the house and spoke with a Mr. Roy, the caretaker. This was the first time Lorraine had ever had a psychic experience...she astrally projected out of her body and hovered above us!

In an interview, Lorraine Warren once provided more detail on her experience at the house: "In that house, I had an out-of-body experience where I could look down and see my husband sitting there and see the man that he was interviewing and see the couple that was with us, but I was way above them. And I could see my own body."

Why the presence of a ghost would cause Lorraine Warren to astral-project is a mystery in itself. In 1959, a friend of Gussie Roy, James Caron, brought a spiritualist named Paul Amsdent to investigate the house. Amsdent reported nothing related to Ocean-Born Mary or Gussie Roy's late mother, as Roy had hoped. He did, however, state that he felt that more than one person was buried around or inside the house.

On the occasion of a second investigation with Amsdent, two women were frightened by the sound of a heavy door opening and closing, seemingly by itself. At about the same time, a man who claimed to be a skeptic about the paranormal was in an upstairs room when, he said, he heard a woman's voice telling him to leave the house.

The accounts of the Amsdent investigations come from the books of Hans Holzer. One the most recognizable names in paranormal research, the Austrian-born Holzer (1920–2009) wrote extensively in several of his books about the so-called Ocean-Born Mary House. He was only vaguely familiar with the story when, in 1963, he received a letter from Corinne Russell, who at the time owned the house with her husband, David.

Holzer retold the Gussie Roy version of the Ocean-Born story in his books as fact, complete with the murder of "Don Pedro" and his burial beneath the hearthstone in the house. He also stated the commonly repeated error that the pirate's real name was Philip Babb, a myth that was established in Lois Lenski's 1939 children's book.

To his credit, Holzer offered the perceptive opinion that the phantom horse-drawn coach described in many versions of the Ocean-Born Mary ghost story was probably borrowed from old Irish folktales. He believed that it had probably been added to Mary's story in recent years.

Corinne Russell told Holzer that she did not want to drive the ghost from the house. "After all," she said, "it *is* her house." She told Holzer that she had not personally seen or felt the presence of any ghosts but that a local medium had seen Mary the first time she visited the house.

Holzer referred to the local medium by the fictitious name "Lorrie" in his books. Lorrie was a Vermont native in her early forties who was living at that

Hans Holzer, Austrian-born paranormal researcher and author. *Courtesy of Alexandra Holzer.*

time in East Weymouth on Boston's South Shore. Holzer contacted Lorrie, who told him that she "would be happy to serve the cause of truth." When Holzer and Lorrie made contact in the winter of 1963, Gussie Roy was still living in an upstairs room in the Henniker mansion he had formerly owned.

Lorrie told Holzer about her first visit to the Henniker house, in September 1961 with her husband and daughter. On that occasion, Gussie Roy showed the family through the house. Nothing happened inside the house, but when they were about to drive away, Lorrie claimed that she saw a woman looking at them for a moment from an upstairs window.

Lorrie said that she watched the woman in the window for about three minutes and described her as "a lovely lady in her thirties, with auburn-colored hair, smiling rather intensely and thoughtfully." The woman in the window was wearing a white dress, Lorrie reported.

Lorrie returned to the house on Halloween in 1961. The word was somehow leaked in advance to the press. Joy Miller of the Associated Press wrote an article that appeared in many newspapers a few days before Halloween, with the headline, "Will Mary Show For Her Portrait?"

Miller's article announced that a psychic would be visiting on Halloween night and that Gussie Roy planned to paint a portrait of Mary based on her description of the ghost. According to Holzer, when Lorrie arrived at the house on Halloween night, she had to sneak in a back door to avoid a crowd of reporters outside.

There was apparently nothing of interest seen on Halloween, but in the following months Lorrie felt a strong urge to return to the house. She returned several times, according to Holzer, and the visits "always left her an emotional wreck." One night, Lorrie had the irresistible urge to drive to Henniker at 11:00 p.m., dressed in her pajamas and a robe. It was as if an unseen force was pulling her to the house. On that particular night, she regained control of herself after driving about ten miles and returned home.

In December 1963, Corinne Russell told Holzer that something interesting had happened since their last conversation. The caretaker of the house had dropped a space heater down the stairs. When it landed at the bottom, kerosene spread and flames quickly shot up the wall. There was no water available, so David Russell rushed out to get some snow. Before he could make it back, Corinne watched the flames go out by themselves. "It was," she told Holzer, "as if someone *had smothered it with a blanket.*"

The Truth Behind a New Hampshire Legend

Other commitments intervened, and Holzer wasn't able to visit the Henniker house with Lorrie until October 1964, just two days before Halloween. In her visits since the sighting of the mysterious woman in the window in 1961, Lorrie said that she hadn't seen any apparitions. But she told Holzer that anytime she touched anything in the house, she received impressions "of what the house was like when Mary had it." Again, it should be pointed out that Mary never lived in the house, and none of the furniture in the house dated back to her lifetime.

Mary "was a quick-tempered woman," Lorrie told Holzer. She felt that Mary was a friendly spirit, but she also claimed to sense the presence of another, more malevolent female ghost in the house—one that grabbed her violently by the arm on one occasion.

According to Holzer, David Russell told him about two odd experiences he'd had in the upstairs room he and Corinne called the Lafayette Room. (This room was named for the French general Lafayette, who supposedly slept there; he most likely never really visited.) Just as he was going to bed one night, David heard heavy footsteps that seemed to be coming from an area on the same floor that had been recently restored.

On another occasion, again as he was getting ready for bed, David heard pounding on the door. A few minutes later, the doorknob began to turn. He opened the door, and there was nobody there. Holzer claimed that the Lafayette Room was where the pirate Don Pedro had lived, which was, of course, based on Gussie Roy's fanciful stories.

Holzer, Lorrie, Lorrie's husband and the Russells seated themselves around the fireplace to see if they could make contact with Ocean-Born Mary. "This was her room," Lorrie claimed, "and I do feel her presence." On the next couple of pages, Holzer described an episode of what is known as automatic writing, as Lorrie put down on paper words that she believed were coming from beyond the grave—from Ocean-Born Mary herself.

Lorrie scrawled a signature, "Mary Wallace," on a piece of paper, and according to Holzer the writing had ornamentation and flourishes "typical of nineteenth century calligraphy" that was nothing like Lorrie's usual small, rounded writing. "She wants me to sleep, but I won't do it," Lorrie announced. Holzer interpreted this as meaning that the ghost wanted to speak through Lorrie, which could only take place if Lorrie went into a trance.

Lorrie finally consented to go into a partial trance. Speaking as if she were someone else, Lorrie said, "She's waiting for Young John. It happened in the north pasture. He killed Warren Langerford. The Frazier boys found the last bone."

At one point during the investigation, according to Holzer, Mary introduced another ghost. "Mrs. Roy is with her, because she killed her daughter, but I don't believe she did," said Lorrie, apparently referring to Gussie Roy's mother. Holzer wrote, "Later we found out the ghost was perhaps not lying, but of course nobody had proof of such a crime—if it were indeed a crime."

Holzer asked Mary, through Lorrie, "Why do you stay in this house?" The answer came quickly, "This is my house, h-o-u-s-e!" When asked if she knew she was dead, Holzer claimed that Mary seemed insulted and withdrew. Holzer and Lorrie gave up on the ghost for that night, somewhat frustrated that no mysteries had been solved.

On another occasion, Lorrie told Holzer, she had been walking around the house, wearing shorts, when she found herself passing through an area full of brambles. "But I never got a scratch," she said, "because I kept feeling heavy skirts covering my legs. I could feel the brambles pulling at this invisible skirt I had on. I felt enveloped by something or someone."

Holzer wrote in *Ghosts of New England* and other books that Lorrie claimed that she felt Ocean-Born Mary's presence in her own home one night, and she expressed the fear that Mary might "get into my body and use it for whatever purpose she wants to. I might wake up some day and *be* Mary Wallace."

Holzer worried that Lorrie had become too consumed by the case, and he decided to bring in an experienced medium with no prior knowledge of Ocean-Born Mary or the house. His choice was Sybil Leek (1917–1982), the famous English psychic, astrologer and author who has been called the "mother of modern witchcraft."

Leek traced her ancestry to Molly Leigh, who had been accused during a sixteenth-century witch hunt. When she was a girl, Leek's family's acquaintances included H.G. Wells and the English occultist Aleister Crowley.

Leek was a high priestess in a coven as a teenager. She eventually authored more than sixty books on occult subjects and became a familiar figure on English television. Her recent biographer, Christine Jones, has called Leek a warm and gentle person who was "like Mother Earth."

The Truth Behind a New Hampshire Legend

For her visit to the so-called Ocean-Born Mary House, Leek brought along her pet boa constrictor, Mr. Sasha, in a basket. "I must confess I found this critter less repulsive than I had thought he would be," wrote Holzer.

After dinner, Holzer, Leek and the Russells went upstairs to the Lafayette Room. Nothing about the house or the Ocean-Born Mary story was discussed with Leek. When asked if she had any initial impressions, Leek said her strongest impressions had been outside, in an area where some irises were planted. "I was drawn to that spot and felt very strange," she said. "There is something outside this house which means more than things inside."

Inside the house, her strongest impression concerned the same upstairs room where a skeptic had said he heard a voice telling him to "get out" years earlier. "They don't want us here," Leek said. "There is a conflict between two people...Somebody wants something he can't have."

Leek then entered a trance, and Holzer waited anxiously for what he anticipated would be the voice of Ocean-Born Mary, speaking from beyond the grave. The first words Leek spoke while in her trance were unintelligible, but they became clearer. "Say-mon go to the lion's head. To the lion's head. Be careful," she said in a cockney accent. Holzer concluded that what sounded like "say-mon" was probably "seaman."

Speaking in the strange cockney dialect, Leek said her name was Mary Degan and that the year was 1798. She said that the house had been built by Daniel Burn, or perhaps Birch. "All the time, come and go...to hide...I have to wait. He wants the money. Burn. Daniel Burn," she said.

Mary Degan lived in the house "with the old idiot," Leek said. When asked who the old idiot was, she said it was "Mary." Holzer asked Mary's family name, and Leek responded, "Birch." Also there, said Leek, was "Jonathan Harrison Flood."

There followed a long stream of fragmentary information from Leek. She said that Burn and Flood were looking for "Dutch gold" that the "old idiot" had taken. The money had belonged to "Johnny," a nickname for Flood, who had been involved in "funny business" at sea. Johnny had been caught, and "they did him in." Mary then hid the money outside, "near the lion's head," which seemed to be rock that resembled the head of a lion.

When asked whose house it was, Leek responded, "Mary Birch." Holzer asked if there was a sea captain in the house, and she almost shouted, "*Johnny!*" She said that Johnny was "from the island." Johnny had met Mary on a ship,

93

she explained. He was buried, she said, "under the fireplace." Holzer asked about the rumors that a pirate was buried under the hearthstone. "Don't tell anyone," Leek whispered. She also hinted that he might not have been dead when he was buried.

As Leek went further off on tangents about "Johnny" and his gold, Holzer decided to try a new tack. "Who was Don Pedro?" he asked. Leek responded that she had heard the name but couldn't place it. When Holzer asked, "What about Mary Wallace?" Leek responded, "Mary Wallace was Mary *Birch*! She had several names." This was because she had several husbands, Leek said. She also said that Mary had four children.

Holzer asked about Philip Babb, whom he wrongly believed was the pirate associated with Mary Wallace's story. "She had a little boy named Philip," Leek said. "Philip Babb, Philip Babb, he was somewhere in the back room. That was his room. I remember him."

The group eventually moved outside, and according to Holzer they were able to find a rock near the irises that indeed resembled a lion's head. He felt that this, along with the talk of a pirate and his treasure and other sketchy correlations, was enough to indicate that Leek's trance-induced stories had been substantially true—never mind the fact that Mary Wallace was married only once and had five children, that she never lived in the house and that Philip Babb had nothing to do with Ocean-Born Mary or the house in Henniker.

Could there be any truth to anything Sybil Leek said on that occasion? Is there anyone or anything of interest buried inside or outside the so-called Ocean-Born Mary House in Henniker? During the years that Gussie Roy owned the house, many people brought in metal detectors and other equipment, and some dug on the grounds. If a treasure hasn't been found by now, it seems doubtful that one ever will be.

Andrew Rothovius, who researched and wrote articles about Ocean-Born Mary in the 1960s, believed that there might have been some validity to Leek's communications, but he thought that they related not to Ocean-Born Mary but rather to the days when the house was possibly used as a center for smuggling. There is no evidence to connect the house to smuggling aside from Rothovius's speculations.

A warning to anyone contemplating a visit to the house with pick and shovel in hand: don't do it. The present owners are entitled to their privacy, and trespassing on their property could land you in jail.

David and Corinne Russell later denied that they ever said that their house was haunted. A reporter in the *Hillsboro Messenger* wrote that the Russells wanted to "expose the myth that the Ocean Born Mary House is haunted; that there were no ghosts there or ever were; and it was just a gimmick to get paying tourists to visit the house."

In her 1967 *Prominent American Ghosts*, Susy Smith said that her inquiries to the Russells were answered by a letter from their lawyer, stating, "Mr. and Mrs. Russell deny that there is any such ghost or other phenomenon associated with the Ocean Born Mary house. Mr. and Mrs. Russell deny the information which you have apparently received from Mr. Holzer's book and further deny that they were instrumental in having him prepare or present any of this information."

Holzer told Smith, "Every word I quoted Mrs. Russell as saying in my book is on tape, there is correspondence where they solicited my coming, etc., on the basis of there being a ghost...but when I last spoke to her she admitted that a lawyer representing a descendant of Mary Wallace had intimidated her and therefore she was changing her story."

It's a likely guess that the Russells, whether or not they experienced anything out of the ordinary in the house themselves, had some fun for a while perpetuating some of Gussie Roy's mythology. Aside from any intimidation by a descendant of Ocean-Born Mary, the fun undoubtedly turned sour when hordes of ghost hunters and treasure seekers consistently turned up at their door day and night. On Halloween night in 1967, it took four Henniker policemen and two firemen to keep traffic moving past the house.

Robert Ellis Cahill, in his booklet *New England's Ghostly Haunts*, wrote:

> *Some of the folks in Henniker believe Mary appears in a horse-drawn black coach every Halloween; some camp out on the doorstep of the house on October 31, waiting for her to arrive in her coach. All who live in the area will agree, the owners in particular, that flying objects bounce off the house on All Hallow's Eve, usually as the evening progresses, but this is not Mary's doings. Those who come to see her begin to hoot and holler when she doesn't appear, and some of the disgruntled ghost-watchers have thrown rocks and other articles at the house, in their frustration at not being haunted.*

According to an article in the *Keene Sentinel* in October 1968, "curiosity seekers, ghost hunters, and threatening vandals" rarely allowed the Russells a good night's sleep. The Russells said that one of them needed to be home at all times to guard against break-ins and vandals.

The Russells were happy to speak to visitors who had a genuine interest in early Americana. "But if they want to hear about ghosts," Corinne said, "forget it." They were always eager to point out that there was solid stone and mortar plainly visible beneath the hearthstone that Gussie Roy always claimed covered the body of the pirate Don Pedro and his treasure.

The Russells hung a sign in the front hall: "About ghosts, apparitions, poltergeists and other assorted such nonsense—we have none." In the early 1970s, when Corinne Russell put the house up for sale, after her husband had died, the realtor advertised the property with the headline, "Ocean Born Mary House, Henniker: The 'spooks' have been evicted but all the charm remains!"

Yankee magazine featured the house in its "House for Sale" column in July 1972. The article, written by *Yankee* editor Judson Hale, stated in no uncertain terms that potential buyers were required to phone ahead for an appointment and that unannounced visitors would be sorry. Some readers showed up without appointments anyway.

Hale later wrote in his book *Inside New England* that there was now a new legend—that the unannounced visitors had been "torn to ribbons by man-eating guard woodchucks." Hale added that the new owners were hoping that the old legends would simply go away, but, as he wrote, "Legends in New England *never* fade away."

The next owners after the Russells, Bob and Mary Gregg, purchased the house after seeing the story in *Yankee*. They owned the house for about a quarter of a century, and they raised four children in it. The Greggs completed much loving restoration, returning the walls to their original colors.

Bob Gregg was once quoted in a newspaper story as saying, "There are no ghosts we know of. The only people we want to see on Halloween night are the neighborhood children."

Is it possible that the mediums who visited the house in the past may have been picking up real information related to genuine people and events from the house's history? Or is it possible that some or all of the information might have been picked up from the subconscious minds of Gussie Roy or others in the house? Your conclusions will largely depend on where you stand on this sort of thing in general.

As for Bob Stamps, the present owner, when asked if he had experienced anything "unusual" in the house, he replied, "Nothing except the squirrels in the walls and the bats in the attic."

Note to would-be ghost hunters: *stay away from the so-called Ocean-Born Mary House*. The owners aren't interested, and it's their house.

THE PIRATE'S TRUE
IDENTITY

Most sources published in the past few decades give the name of the pirate captain in the Ocean-Born Mary story as "Don Pedro." The name seems to have originated in Gussie Roy's 1935 self-published version of the legend, in which he fully admitted that the names he used were fictional.

The term "don," of course, signifies great respect in Spanish. There have been a number of historical figures that may have been referred to as Don Pedro, such as Don Pedro Gonzalvo, an admiral in the Spanish navy in the 1700s.

The most likely inspiration for Roy's use of the name was Don Pedro Gibert (circa 1800–1835), a notorious South American pirate whose base of operations was in south Florida. There was also a Spanish galleon, the *Don Pedro de Montclova*, captured by the pirate captain Ned Low off Cuba in 1723.

Also easily eliminated is Phillip Babb, a real historical figure who lived on the Isles of Shoals off the New Hampshire coast. Lois Lenski, in her 1939 novel *Ocean-Born Mary*, applied Babb's name to the pirate. Lenski appropriated his name simply because of its association with New Hampshire history and legend, and because she liked the sound of it.

Knowing the name of the ship that brought Mary's parents from Ireland might lead us to information on the pirate captain who robbed it. Unfortunately, nobody seems to have recorded the name of the vessel on which Ocean-Born Mary entered the world. In addition, no source provides the name of its captain, the dates of its departure from Ireland or its arrival in New England.

In modern sources, the name of the ship is often given as the *Wolf* or *Wolfe*, but there is no record of a ship with that name arriving from Ireland in that time period. The name never appears in any nineteenth-century tellings of the story.

The 1910 book *Scotch Irish Pioneers in Ulster and America*, by Charles Knowles Bolton, tells us that several ships arrived in New England from Ireland in the summer of 1720. Two of the listings mention that pirates took the ships, which immediately makes them suspects in the Ocean-Born Mary story. They are described as follows:

> [Name not given], *Benjamin Marston, master, from Ireland; arr. Aug., at Salem. Taken by pirates. Had several passengers.*
>
> *Essex, brigantine, Robert Peat, master, from Ireland; arr. July?, at Salem. Held up by Capt. Thomas Roberts, a pirate.*

The *Boston News-Letter* of August 22–29, 1720, printed an account of Benjamin Marston Jr.'s adventures aboard an unnamed ship voyaging from Ireland to New England:

> *Last week arrived at Salem Capt. Marston from Ireland with several Passengers, both Men and Women, who [were] taken by Captain Roberts, the Pirate, about two Days after he had parted from Captain Carey. The said Pirate had also taken a Bristol vessel bound for Virginia from Bristol, out of whom the Pirate took his goods and Forced some or most of his Men, and put on board several of Captain Marston's Men or Passengers to go with her for Bristol.*

It would appear that the ship in this report is the first of the two from Bolton's list, cited above. But a look at the *Memoirs of the Marstons of Salem* indicates that Benjamin Marston Jr. was aboard the *Essex*, which left Ireland on June 16, 1720. From this information, we can deduce that the two ships said by Bolton to have had encounters with pirates are, in fact, the same ship—the *Essex*.

Bolton's confusion probably stemmed from the fact that the August 22–29 *News-Letter* referred to Marston as the captain of the ship, which was unnamed in the account. Other accounts from about the same time named

Robert Peat as the captain of the *Essex*. It's not hard to understand why Bolton thought they were two separate vessels. The *News-Letter* was in error in the account quoted above; Marston was the owner and not the captain of the *Essex*.

A little background on Marston adds even more poignancy to the story of the *Essex*'s fateful 1720 voyage. Benjamin Marston Sr. (1651–1719), was a prominent Salem merchant and church deacon. He sailed with his son aboard the *Essex* to Ireland in late summer 1719, arriving in Kinsale on September 7. Not long after that, the elder Marston was stricken with smallpox.

In November, Benjamin Jr. wrote to his mother:

> *This comes with unwelcome news of the Death of my Father, who was taken with ye Smal-pox and died in about Ten days after Our arrival: the night he died I was taken ill of the same distemper and was dangerously sick, but by God's providence recovered, and am in good health.*

Twenty-two-year-old Benjamin Marston Jr., a 1715 graduate of Harvard, unexpectedly found himself in charge of the affairs of the *Essex* after his father's death. He wrote to his mother on March 5, 1720:

> *I did expect to have been at Sea by this day but was disappointed in my passengers. I am now ready to Sail from this place to London Derry but yt I wait for about 30 passengers which I expect on board next week, and at Derry [Londonderry] I hope to make up the Complement of 100. So that I do not expect to Sail for N. England till ye 10th of April if then. I have paid off the Bill, according to agreemt which, with ye fitting out of ye Ship, & Our great expense here this Six months will very much hinder Our making a good Voyage, tho I hope, with God's blessing, We Shall make a Saving Voyage.*

The *Essex* finally sailed from Dublin, probably by early June, and it proceeded up Ireland's east coast to Londonderry. In late July, word reached Salem that the *Essex* "was cast away and all on board drowned." Soon after, it was reported in the *Boston News-Letter* of August 1–8 that "the said Briganteen was stranded and is since safely arrived at London-Derry without any person being lost."

The Truth Behind a New Hampshire Legend

At Londonderry, additional passengers boarded the brigantine for the crossing to New England. Could this be the ship and the voyage of the Ocean-Born Mary story?

We have more descriptions of the eventful journey of the *Essex*. The following account is given in *Memoirs of the Marstons of Salem*, possibly quoting a newspaper of the time:

> On the 22nd of August 1720, the Essex reached Salem, "after a long and stormy passage of 67 days, in which they encountered many disasters." Previous to her arrival, there had been rumors of her having been taken by pirates.

The *Boston News-Letter* of August 22–29, 1720, published more detail of the *Essex*'s encounter with pirates. The attack took place at 4:00 a.m., according to the *News-Letter*:

> The briganteen Essex was taken by Two Pirates, one a French Built Ship of about Two Hundred and Twenty Tons, Twenty-six guns mounted, and One hundred Men, Commanded by one Roberts, the other a Sloop of about Eighty Tons, Ten Guns mounted, and ----- men, who did him considerable Damage, and abused several Women that was Passengers on Board... The pirates declared they would have sunk Capt. Peates Briganteen if they could have known what to have done with his Servants and Passengers; the next Day being the 18 about Two a Clock they parted with him, and said they designed for Madera.

The meaning of "abused" here isn't clear; pirates sometimes raped non-European women on ships they captured, but rarely white women.

The following statement was made in an Essex County court on August 31, 1720:

> Capt. Robert Peat, commander of the Brigg Essex, made declaration that they sailed, June 16, 1720, from Londonderrey, Ireland, bound for New England and having on board 100 passengers, men, women and children, beside the ships crew, and on July 17th, when they were about 60 leagues eastward of Newfoundland Banks in lat. 43° 40' "there came up with

them a pyrat ship mannd with about 100 hands Capt. Roberts, its leader
& a sloop with about forty more & boarded them & took them & plundered
& Ruled them of almost all that was worth taking Even thier very wearing
apparell & put ym in great Terrour of thier Lives by holding a pistol at
thier breasts & Telling them they should have no quarter & tooke away
most of thier Saylers Rifled thier Cabin Stateroom & Hold & damnifyed
thier vessel considerably."

The *Boston News-Letter* of October 10–17, 1720, published this additional item concerning the *Essex:*

Daniel Starr of Boston, by Trade a Joyner, but lately a Mariner on board
the Briganteen Essex, whereof Robert Peat was Commander, [related
that] *in his Voyage from Ireland to Salem on the 17th of July last he*
was taken by one Captain Thomas Roberts, Commander of a Pirate ship
and sloop of 150 men, and forced the said Starr to go along with him
against his will.

A similar report on Daniel Starr's misfortune in the *American Weekly Mercury* referred to the pirate as "John Roberts."

Meanwhile, John Leverett, president of Harvard College and a friend of the Marstons, wrote to Patience Marston, who was Benjamin Marston Jr.'s mother and herself the daughter of a former Harvard president:

I have bin in pain for yor Son ever since I had the acct of Captn. Cary's
disaster, and it wd have added to my rejoicing had your Son escaped those
enormous Creatures [pirates]. *However, I can't suffer his misfortune to*
diminish my hearty acknowledgmt of the Divine favour in bringg the dear
Youth to you alive and in health, after all the fears and Concerns We have
had about him.

None of these reports of the *Essex*'s encounter with pirates mentions anything about a baby having been born on the voyage or about the pirate captain sparing the lives of the passengers because of the presence of an infant. But there are many other factors that suggest that Mary was born on the *Essex* and that the contemporary reports of the pirate attack on July 17 are describing the same event described in the Ocean-Born Mary story.

The accounts state that the pirates boarded the *Essex* on July 17, and tradition tells us that Mary was born eleven days later on July 28. There's an essential factor that might resolve this discrepancy. When Mary was born, much of the world was still using the Julian (old style) calendar. The Gregorian (new style) calendar had been created and adopted in many countries in 1582, but England (and presumably the Ulster Scots) and its American colonies didn't officially adopt the reformed calendar until 1752. In order to make the calendar adjustment in England and the American colonies, eleven days were dropped from the month of September 1752.

A check of the *Boston News-Letter* in 1720 indicates that they were still using the old style of dating; for instance, the edition of July 17, 1720, was published on a Sunday. July 17 would be a Wednesday on the Gregorian calendar. The *News-Letter* didn't begin adding eleven days to the dates until 1752.

Thus, the reported date of July 17 in the *News-Letter* for the pirate assault on the *Essex* translates to July 28 in the new style.

The earliest published versions of the Ocean-Born Mary story, including the 1849 newspaper account and Edward L. Parker's 1851 *History of Londonderry*, don't provide a date for Mary's birth other than the year 1720. The earliest publishing I've found of her birth date as July 28, 1720, is in the 1901 *History of Milford*, in a biography of Mary's descendant Robert Moore Wallace.

We have no contemporary accounts of the subsequent celebrations of Mary's birthday in Londonderry, New Hampshire. All we know is that, according to accounts published much later, her birthday was celebrated on July 28. If this date is new style dating, it means she was born on July 17, old style.

Perhaps Mary and/or her family, sometime after 1752, converted the original date of July 17 to the new calendar. To do that, they would have added eleven days, making it July 28, 1720.

In his daybook, on the day his mother died (February 13, 1814), Mary's son William Wallace wrote: "My Honored Mother Departed this Life at 6 O'Clock in the Evening. Aged Ninety Three Years Six Months and twenty seven days."

Subtracting ninety-three years, six months, and twenty-seven days from February 13, 1814, gives us a result of July 17, 1720. Adding the eleven days that were subtracted from the calendar in 1752 gives us a result of July 28, 1720, new style.

A nineteenth- or early twentieth-century researcher may have picked up the date of Mary's birth from the information William wrote when his mother died. The researcher would thus have figured her birth date to be July 28, 1720, new style. Once it was in writing, the date of July 28 could easily have been copied in subsequent accounts.

If this theory about Mary's birth date is correct, there would appear to be a strong likelihood that Mary was born aboard the *Essex* on July 17, 1720, and that the ship was boarded by Captain Roberts and his crew on the day she was born.

According to the theory, here is the timeline of the voyage of the *Essex*:

May or June?	Leaves Dublin, runs into a delay on the way to Londonderry to pick up passengers.
June 16, 1720	Leaves Londonderry with about one hundred passengers.
July 17, 1720	Mary is born, and pirates board and plunder the ship.
August 22, 1720	Arrives in Salem, Massachusetts.

If this is the correct scenario, it dovetails nicely with the versions of the story that claim that Mary had just been born when the pirates were encountered or that she was born while the pirates were on board.

Accounts published in 1849 and 1876 state that Mary was born prematurely while the ship was in the hands of the pirates. Medical research indicates that a traumatic event—and a pirate attack certainly qualifies as one—can trigger early labor and a premature birth.

It seems safe to assume that Elizabeth Wilson would not have chosen to give birth at sea. Let's say she left Ireland when she was six to seven months pregnant. She would have had every expectation that the voyage would end in New England in about six weeks and that she would give birth after the voyage. The pirate encounter and Mary's birth took place one month into the voyage, meaning that she would have been seven or eight months pregnant. The baby would have been premature but would have had a good chance of survival.

The *Boston News-Letter* of August 22–29, 1720, reported that Roberts and his crew stayed with the *Essex* from 4:00 a.m. on July 17 until 2:00 (a.m.

or p.m.) on July 18. That would certainly have allowed plenty of time for Mary's birth and the subsequent events described in so many versions of the Ocean-Born Mary story.

The report by Captain Peat states that the pirates took "almost all that was worth taking" from the passengers on the *Essex*. According to the earliest known published account of the Ocean-Born Mary story, the 1849 newspaper article, the pirates allowed the passengers to "proceed on their voyage with all their effects, save a few muskets and some ammunition which the pirates retained." It seems possible that Peat's account was exaggerated or that the 1849 account was inaccurate on that detail. It also seems possible that the pirates might have taken everything from the crew but left the passengers alone.

The voyage of the *Essex* took sixty-seven days. It was described in a newspaper account as "long and stormy," which meshes with some early versions of the Ocean-Born Mary story. The pirate attack on the *Essex* took place a little less than halfway through the voyage (in terms of time rather than distance), which isn't so different from William Thyng's 1906 assertion that the attack occurred about one-third of the way through the voyage.

It's been frequently stated that Mary's ship arrived in Boston, while the voyage of the *Essex* ended in Salem. The two cities are only about a dozen miles from each other, making this a minor point.

All in all, it seems that a good case can be made for the *Essex* as the ship and Captain Roberts as the pirate in the Ocean-Born Mary story—maybe not an airtight case, but certainly a strong one.

So who was this Captain Roberts mentioned in the accounts of the pirate attack on the *Essex*? Although he's referred to as Thomas Roberts in some accounts, he was undoubtedly the Welsh-born Bartholomew Roberts—the most successful pirate captain in the Golden Age of Piracy. Roberts captured far more ships than his more famous contemporaries, including Captain Kidd and Blackbeard. Between 1719 and 1722, Roberts took well over four hundred craft.

"Thomas Roberts" is cited as a pseudonym of Bartholomew Roberts in several sources. Aubrey Burl's book *Black Barty* tells us that Thomas Roberts was "an amalgam of Thomas Anstis and Bartholomew Roberts, of quartermaster and captain." Roberts is frequently referred to as "Black Bart" in modern sources, but that name was not used in his lifetime.

In the summer of 1720, Roberts and his crew were blazing a trail of terror around Newfoundland. In late June, they raided the large harbor at Trepassey, easily taking control of the harbor and twenty-two ships. The *Weekly Journal or British Gazetteer* reported that Roberts "made the masters all prisoners and beat some of them heartily for their cowardice for not making any resistance." One of the captains was tied to a mast and flogged mercilessly.

The pirate flotilla then headed out into the Atlantic about two hundred miles southeast of Newfoundland, where they waited for easy prey: fishing boats, merchant ships and immigrant ships. The flagship of Roberts's fleet was the twenty-six-gun *Good Fortune*, a captured French warship.

The *Boston News-Letter* of August 22–29, 1720, mentions that Captain Roberts attacked Benjamin Marston's ship after he had taken a vessel under the command of Captain Carey. The *Samuel* was the vessel in question, under the command of Captain Samuel Carey. It was taken by Roberts and about one hundred men on July 13, some forty miles east of the Newfoundland Banks. The *Samuel* had left London eleven weeks earlier.

A circa 1724 illustration by Benjamin Cole of Bartholomew Roberts, the most successful pirate who ever lived.

The Truth Behind a New Hampshire Legend

The *Boston News-Letter* later provided a detailed description of what had transpired aboard the *Samuel*, which gives us an idea of what Mary's parents and their fellow passengers might have endured when the *Essex* was boarded by Roberts and his men:

> *The first thing the Pirates did, was to strip both Passengers and Seamen of all their Money and Cloths which they had on board, with a loaded Pistol held to every ones breast ready to shoot him down, who did not immediately give an account of both, and resign them up. The next thing they did was, with madness and rage to tare up the Hatches, enter the Hould like a parcel of Furies, where with Axes, Cutlashes, etc., they cut, tore and broke open Trunks, Boxes, Cases and Bales, and when any of the Goods came upon Deck which they did not like to carry with them aboard their Ship, instead of tossing them into the Hould again they threw them over board into the Sea. The usual method they had to open Chests was by shooting a brace of Bullets with a Pistol into the Key-hole to force them open. The Pirates carryed away from Capt. Carry's Ship aboard their own 40 barrels of Powder, two great Guns, his Cables, &c. and to the value of about nine or ten Thousand Pounds Sterling worth of the Choicest Goods he had on board. There was nothing heard among the Pirates all the while, but Cursing, Swearing, Dam'ing and Blaspheming to the greatest degree imaginable, and often saying they would not go to Hope point in the River of Thames to be hung up in Gibbets a Sundrying as Kidd and Bradish's Company did, for if it should chance that they should be Attacked by any Superiour power or force, which they could not master, they would immediately put fire with one of their Pistols to their Powder, and go all merrily to Hell together!...Whilst the Pirates were disputing whither to sink or burn Capt. Carry's Ship they spy'd a sail that same evening, and so let him go free.*

In his 1724 volume *A General History of the Pyrates*, Captain Charles Johnson provided a similar description of the ransacking of the *Samuel*, adding, "The *Samuel* was a rich ship, and had several Passengers on board who were used very roughly, in order to make them discover their Money, threatening them every Moment with Death, if they did not resign every Thing up to them."

Roberts took more ships within days of the *Samuel*, including the *Little York* from Virginia, the *Love* of Liverpool, the *Phoenix* of Bristol, an unnamed brigantine and a sloop called the *Sadbury*. The pirates sank the brigantine after the men had been removed. "Day after day," according to Aubrey Burl, "vessels appeared, hove to, were ransacked without bloodshed and released after yielding a few more precious trinkets, barrels, coins and provisions. The Newfoundland coast was a garden of plenty."

According to some estimates, Roberts's crew boarded as many as 170 vessels during this period. By July 19, Roberts and his men were sailing south, leaving the waters off Newfoundland far behind.

It seems useful to examine the known facts about Bartholomew Roberts as they relate to other aspects of the Ocean-Born Mary story. He was born a few miles from the sea in the village of Casnewydd-Bach (Little Newcastle), southwestern Wales, in 1682, and his real name was John Roberts or Robert. It's believed that his father was named George Robert, but his mother's name is unknown.

The earliest published versions of the Ocean-Born Mary story claim that the pirate captain was himself a father and that he wanted the newborn infant to be named Mary for his own wife. Other versions say Mary was the pirate's mother's name, and still others leave it ambiguous.

Roberts doesn't seem to have married or to have had children; at least one biographer has written that it's likely that Roberts was gay, though others dispute that. Considering the kind of life he led as a sailor and a pirate, the possibility of Roberts fathering a child can't be ruled out.

Roberts's mother could very easily have been named Mary. The name enjoyed great popularity in England after the start of the Reformation; about 15–20 percent of women were named Mary in the late 1600s. Figures for Wales for that period are uncertain, but census data shows 23.9 percent of females in Wales named Mary in 1800; it was the most common female name.

Roberts went to sea at thirteen and sailed as a merchant until 1719. When he was forced to join a pirate crew in 1719 under the notorious captain Howell Davis, he resisted at first. But Roberts quickly recognized the benefits of piracy. Captain Charles Johnson quoted him:

> *In an honest service there is thin commons, low wages, and hard labour.*
> *In this, plenty and satiety, pleasure and ease, liberty and power. And who*

would not balance creditor on this side, when all the hazard that is run for it, at worst is only a sour look or two at choking? No, a merry life and a short one shall be my motto.

Roberts was chosen as captain when Davis was killed, after a mere six weeks as a pirate. He was chosen because he exceeded the other crewmen in "knowledge and boldness" and was able to "make those fear who do not love him." Roberts said, "If a Pirate I must be, 'tis better being a Commander than a common Man." He adopted "Bartholomew" as his pirate name, possibly in honor of a prominent buccaneer of the 1680s named Bartholomew Sharp.

In his pirating days, Roberts was described as tall, stout and swarthy. He preferred drinking tea to wine, and he enjoyed wearing gentleman's clothes, such as a bright crimson waistcoat and breeches, a cocked hat with a red feather and a heavy gold necklace with a diamond cross.

Aubrey Burl wrote that the pirates under Roberts leveled pistols at the crew of the *Samuel* in a "pretense of intimidation," suggesting that the bark of Roberts and his men was worse than their bite. But Roberts certainly wasn't averse to violence. As David Cordingly wrote in his book *Under the Black Flag*, Roberts "had no qualms about resorting to torture and murder to achieve his ends." It's commonly repeated that Roberts once had a ship burned with eighty slaves on board, but that incident may have been the work of another pirate on his crew.

In any case, if the pirates held pistols to the *Essex* passengers' chests and threatened them, as reported, they must have believed that their lives were in great jeopardy.

As with most of the pirates in the Golden Age of Piracy, much of the information we have on Roberts comes from the seminal 1724 book *A General History of the Pyrates* by Captain Charles Johnson. Johnson stressed that if Roberts sometimes treated his victims well, he also told them that it was "pure inclination that induced him to a good treatment of them, and not any love or partiality to their persons."

According to many sources, Roberts sometimes gave gifts, such as jewelry or items of captured cargo, to cooperative captains and crews of captured ships. This matches up nicely with the tradition that Mary's mother was presented with silk and other gifts from the pirate captain.

There was an intriguing passage in the *News-Letter* of August 15–22, 1720, following the account of the taking of the *Samuel*: "Roberts the Pirate says,

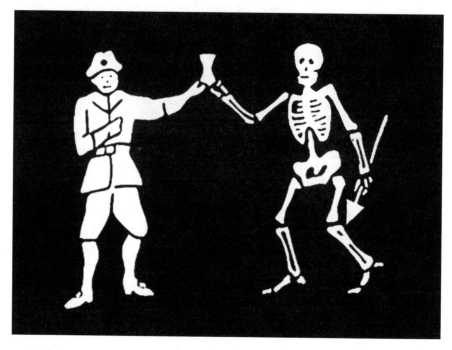

The Jolly Roger of pirate captain Bartholomew Roberts. *Illustration by Olek Remesz, Wikimedia Commons.*

that there is a French Pirate on the North Coast of America, who gives no Quarter to any Nation, and if he met him, he would give him none."

Could this unnamed Frenchman be the pirate who figured in the Ocean-Born Mary story? One of the best-known French pirates at the time was Olivier Levasseur, also known as Olivier La Bouche. He was known to be off the east coast of Africa on July 25, 1720, so it seems unlikely that he could have been the pirate who attacked Mary's ship in the Atlantic.

There was also a French pirate from Saint-Malo named Montigny La Palisse, who had joined with Roberts in the Caribbean in February 1720. La Palisse fled during a battle with British naval ships near Barbados but rejoined Roberts after the raid on Trepassey, Newfoundland. V'léOnica Roberts, author of *Captain Bartholomew Roberts: A Pirate's Journal* and a student of pirate history, believes that the twenty-six-gun ship that was taken by Roberts and renamed *Good Fortune* was actually taken from La Palisse and that the Frenchman was put in charge of a smaller ship under Roberts.

Later, after the pirate fleet had left Newfoundland and returned to the Caribbean in July 1720, it's recorded that La Palisse was commanding the *Good Fortune* under Roberts.

The *Boston News-Letter* of August 22–29, 1720, mentions "two pirates" and two ships in the attack on the *Essex*. The "French Built ship" with twenty-six guns described in the account is undoubtedly the *Good Fortune* under Roberts. The sloop mentioned in the account could have been La Palisse's vessel.

It's possible that Montigny La Palisse might have been the pirate of the Ocean-Born Mary story. Unfortunately, we have scant information about La Palisse; what little we know is based strictly on his association with Roberts.

V'léOnica Roberts speculates that it might have been La Palisse who threatened the passengers aboard the *Essex* and Roberts who let them go free, "perhaps using the female child as his excuse."

Before heading to Newfoundland, Roberts and his fleet carried out much successful plundering in the West Indies. After leaving Newfoundland, Roberts returned to the Caribbean and promptly hanged the governor of Martinique from the yardarm of his flagship to settle a previous score. Roberts's fleet grew so large and powerful by the spring of 1721 that commerce virtually stopped. At the height of his career, Roberts was in command of more than five hundred men.

Captain Bartholomew Roberts also used this flag, showing him standing on two skulls; the initials stand for "A Barbadian's Head" and "A Martiniquian's Head" after the Caribbean islands of Barbados and Martinique. *Illustration by Olek Remesz, Wikimedia Commons.*

Roberts was shot and killed in battle on February 10, 1722, off the west coast of Africa. He was buried at sea by his men, as he had requested. His death is often cited as the end of the Golden Age of Piracy.

Assuming that the theory about Mary's birth on July 17 aboard the *Essex* isn't foolproof, let's look at other possibilities. There's sketchy information on two or three other vessels from Ireland that arrived in Boston or nearby ports in the summer of 1720. There don't seem to be any contemporary reports of pirate attacks during these voyages, but that doesn't mean that such events didn't occur.

There was plenty of piracy to go around in 1720. Estimates of the number of pirates active at that time run as high as 2,400 men. The majority, however, were primarily active in the Caribbean Sea and the Indian Ocean. Piracy had been rampant around the British Isles, particularly in the sixteenth and early seventeenth centuries, but improved laws for trying pirates greatly reduced the amount of piratical activity in the vicinity by about 1700.

Other pirates, including Thomas Anstis and John Phillips, were active off Newfoundland about 1721–23. In fact, for a brief period in the early 1720s, Newfoundland was a stopover point for a number of pirates who raided shipping in the North Atlantic. But nowhere—at least not in the course of the research for this book—does there appear any evidence that ships leaving Ireland were robbed on their way to North America in the summer of 1720 by pirates other than Bartholomew Roberts and his underlings.

Even if the Wilsons were aboard a ship other than the *Essex*, it still seems likely that Roberts or La Palisse—or perhaps another pirate acting on behalf of Roberts—was the pirate of the Ocean-Born Mary story.

THE BOTTOM LINE

The legend of Ocean-Born Mary may be famous, but only fragmentary descriptions of the real Mary have survived, and we're not apt to fill the gaps with any new information at this late date. Perhaps future historians will find some missing pieces to Mary's story that may have eluded me. More likely, we'll have to be content to rely on our imaginations to bring her to life.

On the other hand, we know plenty about Gussie Roy. He piggybacked the Ocean-Born Mary story to some degree of fame and took advantage of a gullible media, but his wild stories stirred imaginations and helped to put Henniker on the map. The story might have been mostly forgotten if not for Roy's imaginative promotions.

There's also no doubt that Roy was a photographer of considerable ability. As Martha C. Taylor of the Henniker Historical Society has written, "His photographs and article documenting old ways of working are a significant contribution to our understanding of an earlier time."

The theory regarding the identity of the ship and the pirate captain in the story can't be proven, but it looks like a mountain of circumstantial evidence points to Bartholomew Roberts or a cohort.

There's still plenty of room for speculation and romance. What was it about the sight of a newborn baby girl that stirred such tender feelings in a hardened pirate captain? Who was the pirate's beloved Mary, for whom Mary Wilson was named?

Ocean-Born Mary continues to enthrall new generations, and the story's influence sometimes crops up in unexpected places. The rock musician Keith Emerson—of Emerson, Lake and Palmer fame—released a 2009 album that included a conceptual suite entitled "The House of Ocean-Born Mary."

A New England folk-singing duo, Neptune's Car, has also recorded a song inspired by the legend. The lyrics include this lovely chorus:

> *It was your destiny to be*
> *Born upon the sea*
> *Named by a man with a cutlass sword*
> *Once your mother gave her word.*

It seems fitting to end with two quotes. First, the words of Gussie Roy's friend, Paul S. Scruton, who wrote the following a few years after Roy's death:

> *As the sun sinks in the west and darkness soon follows, the Ocean Born Mary House is still in the shadows at eveningtide. But nothing strange seems to have happened there in more recent years—and if phantoms*

The Center Cemetery in Henniker, final resting place of Ocean-Born Mary. *Photo by Jeremy D'Entremont.*

walk abroad nobody pays attention any more. And even Gussie has not been seen since his departure from this mundane sphere.

And finally, the only quote we have from Ocean-Born Mary herself:

Indeed, I was born neither on this side or that side o' the water, nor anywhere else on God's green earth.

"THE ROMANCE OF 'OCEAN MARY'"

J. Warren Thyng

1906

PREVIOUS to 1720, the year in which the principal events of this narrative occurred, many families of Scotch peasantry crossed the North Channel and found, for a time, homes in the larger towns on or near the coast of Ireland. Thus Londonderry became the residence of a large number of Scotch yeomanry.

In those old times of slow ships and many perils of the sea, it was a far cry from Londonderry in Ireland to Londonderry in the Granite State; still Scotland and the Emerald Isle had already sent sturdy pioneers to the new world on the Merrimack.

Tradition, often the truer part of history, has failed to save from oblivion the name of the ship which sailed from Londonderry for Boston in July, 1720, but she is said to have been in many respects vastly superior to others of her class in those times. At any rate, long before she dropped anchor off the picturesque coast, many well-to-do families had prepared for the long voyage. Of those who from the deck of the departing ship watched the green shores of Ireland fade from view, a large proportion were not only strong of limb, but thrifty and provident.

Out through Lough Foye, past Inishowen Head and far beyond Giant's Causeway, with favoring winds, sailed the fated ship.

Among the passengers were James Wilson and his young wife. A year before Wilson married Elizabeth Fulton, and they were now on their way to

Londonderry, N.H., where land had been laid out to James Wilson as one of the grantees of that town.

In the small valley settlement to which Wilson and his wife were traveling were friends under whose hands profitable harvests were sure, and a generation was springing up whose influence was to be felt long years after.

Concerning the earlier part of the voyage of the emigrant ship, tradition is nearly silent, although certain fragmentary accounts hint of a protracted calm and following storm of such violence that the vessel was driven from her course. However that may be, it is reasonably certain that the passage was about one third accomplished when events transpired that made the voyage memorable in the lives of all on board.

One sultry evening the lookout saw on the horizon a sail standing like a gray silhouette against the early rising moon. All through the hot summer night the strange craft wore nearer and nearer, and when morning came her low hull could be seen like a black shadow under her full set of canvas.

The pirate was within gunshot of the emigrant ship. To fight or run away was not to be thought of. The slow ship had not a dozen muskets. They simply waited. They had not long to wait, for boats were soon alongside and, swarming upon the deck, the robbers fell to work as men who knew how to plunder and kill. Crew and passengers were bound, and some were left lying where they were captured, and some were rolled into corners, just as suited a momentary freak of the invaders.

None were killed. Valuables were gathered into parcels convenient to be transferred to the pirate ship. The robber captain, going below to search the officers' quarters, threw open the after-cabin door with a rough hand, but seeing a woman lying in the berth, stopped.

"Why are you there?" demanded the ruffian.

"See." The terrified woman uncovered a baby's face.

Then the pirate drew near. "Is it a boy or a girl?"

"A girl."

"Have you named her?"

"No."

The pirate went to the cabin door and commanded that no man stir until further orders. Then, returning, he went close to the berth where the woman lay, and said gently, "If I may name that baby, that little girl, I will unbind your men and leave your ship unharmed. May I name the girl?"

"Yes."

Then the rough old robber came nearer still and took up the tiny, unresisting hand of the baby. "Mary," was the name the woman heard him speak. There were other words, but spoken so low she could not hear. Only his Maker and his own heart knew, but when the child drew its hand away the mother saw a tear on the pink fingers.

There have been other knights than Bayard. Here was one.

As good as his word, the pirate captain ordered all captives unbound, and goods and valuables restored to the places from which they had been taken; then with his crew he left the ship and pulled to his own vessel. But the emigrant ship had scarcely got under way when a new alarm came to them. The pirate was returning.

If they were dismayed at his reappearance, they were surprised to see him come on board alone and go directly below to the cabin. There he took from a parcel a piece of brocaded silk of marvelous fineness of texture and beauty of design.

Time has, perhaps, somewhat mellowed its color tone, but the richness of its quality is as the richness of pearls.

"Let Mary wear this on her wedding day," the pirate said as he laid the silk on the berth.

The pirate left the ship and was seen no more. In the fullness of time the emigrant ship reached Boston without further incident. There James Wilson died soon after landing. Elizabeth Wilson, with Mary, soon after went to live in Londonderry, where friends were waiting for them. Here the widow married James Clark, great-great-grandparent of Horace Greeley.

For years the people of the little hamlet religiously kept July 28, in thanksgiving for the deliverance of their friends from the hands of pirates.

Some time early in the year 1738, Thomas Wallace emigrated to America and settled in Londonderry, where, on December 18 of the same year, he was married to Ocean Mary by Rev. Mr. Davidson of that town. Her wedding gown was the pirate's silk. [Note: Mary married Thomas Wallace's son, James, in 1742.]

A granddaughter and a great-granddaughter have also worn the same dress on like occasions.

Four sons were born to Mary Wallace, three of whom removed to Henniker. There, on a sightly hill, Robert built the house which in his day was far and away the grandest mansion in all the country around. He was a man of large hospitality and intelligent strength of character.

Here Ocean Mary lived many years, and died in 1814 at the age of ninety-four years. Her grave is in the Center burying ground, about half way down the middle walk, a bowshot distant from the railroad station. The curious visitor may, if he choose, read the inscription on the slate: "In Memory of Widow Mary Wallace, who died Feb'y 13, A.D., 1814, in the 94th year of her age."

The likeness tradition has left of Ocean Mary is that of a woman symmetrically tall, with light hair, blue eyes and florid complexion, together with a touch of the aristocracy of nature and a fine repose of manner in her energetic, determined and kindly ways.

The house is four miles from Henniker village and about the same distance from Hillsborough. The visitor, if he have an eye for the picturesque, though he regret the decay that has overtaken the old manse, can but be charmed by the beauty of the landscape in the midst of which it is set.

SELECTED BIBLIOGRAPHY

Adams, Ida G. "An Historical Romance." *Granite Monthly* 25 (1898).

Botkin, B.A. *A Treasury of New England Folklore*. New York: Crown, 1947.

Breverton, Terry. *Black Bart Roberts: The Greatest Pirate of Them All*. Gretna, LA: Pelican, 2004.

Browne, George Waldo. *Early Records of Londonderry, Windham, and Derry, N.H., 1719–1762*. Manchester, NH: John B. Clarke, 1908.

Browne, George Waldo, ed. *Vital Records of Londonderry, New Hampshire., 1719–1762*. Manchester, NH: Manchester Historic Association, 1914.

Burl, Aubrey. *Black Barty: Bartholomew Roberts and His Pirate Crew, 1718–1723*. Phoenix Mill, UK: Sutton Publishing, 1997.

Cahill, Robert Ellis. *New England's Ghostly Haunts*. Peabody, MA: Chandler-Smith, 1983.

Carmer, Carl. *The Hurricane's Children*. New York: David McKay, 1937.

Cogswell, Leander Winslow. *History of the Town of Henniker*. Concord, NH: Republican Press Association, 1880.

Cordingly, David. *Under the Black Flag*. New York: Harcourt Brace, 1997.

Cutter, Richard William, ed. *Genealogical and Family History of Western New York*. New York: Lewis Historical Publishing Company, 1912.

D'Agostino, Thomas. *Haunted New Hampshire*. Atglen, PA: Schiffer, 2006.

Doty, Lockwood Lyon. *A History of Livingston County, New York*. Geneseo, NY: Edward E. Doty, 1876.

Drury, John. *The Heritage of Early American Houses*. New York: Coward-McCann, 1969.

Essex Institute. *Essex Institute Historical Collections*. Vol. 44. Salem, MA: Essex Institute, 1908.

Flanders, Alice V., and Martha C. Taylor. *Ocean Born Mary and Mr. Roy: Linked by Legend*. Henniker, NH: Henniker Historical Society, 2000.

Garvin, James L. *A Building History of Northern New England*. Lebanon, NH: University Press of New England, 2001.

Hale, Judson. *Inside New England*. New York: Harper and Row, 1982.

Hill, Edwin L. "A History of Photography in LaCrosse, Wisconsin, 1853–1930." Thesis, University of Wisconsin–La Crosse, 1978.

Holden, Raymond P. *The Merrimack*. Toronto: Clarke, Irwin & Company, 1958.

Holmes, Richard. *Nutfield Rambles*. Portsmouth, NH: Peter E. Randall, 2007.

Holzer, Hans. *America's Haunted Houses*. Stamford, CT: Longmeadow Press, 1991.

———. *Ghosts of New England.* New York: Wings Books, 1996.

———. *Great American Ghost Stories.* New York: Dorset, 1963.

Howells, John Mead. *Architectural Heritage of the Merrimack.* New York: Architectural Book Publishing Company, 1941.

Johnson, Charles. *A General History of the Robberies & Murders of the Most Notorious Pirates.* Guilford, CT: Lyons Press, 2002, originally published 1724.

Jones, Eric. *New Hampshire Curiosities.* Guilford, CT: Morris Book Publishing, 2006.

Konstam, Angus, with Roger Michael Kean. *Pirates: Predators of the Seas.* New York: Skyhorse, 2007.

Lenski, Lois. *Ocean-Born Mary.* New York: Stokes, 1939.

Lowndes, Marion. *Ghosts that Still Walk.* New York: Alfred A. Knopf, 1941.

Mack, Robert C. *The Londonderry Celebration: Exercises on the 150th Anniversary of the Settlement of Old Nutfield.* Manchester, NH: John B. Clarke, 1869.

Newton, Jim. "A Biography of Ocean-Born Mary." Concord, New Hampshire, 1953. Typescript copy at the Henniker Historical Society.

Parker, Edward L., Reverend. *The History of Londonderry, Comprising the Towns of Derry and Londonderry, N.H.* Boston, MA: Perkins and Whipple, 1851.

Portsmouth Journal. "A Scotch Irish Family of N. Hampshire." February 24, 1849.

Richmond, Robert P. "Ghost Keeper." *New Hampshire Profiles,* March 1963.

Roberts, Eleanor. "Ghost of Ocean-Born Mary, Driving Coach and Four, Is Due to Appear in Henniker, N.H., this Month." *Boston Sunday Post,* October 2, 1938.

Rothovius, Andrew. "Historic Henniker Mansion Still Has Its Share of Mystery." *Milford Cabinet*, April 13, 1967.

———. "Ocean Born Mary: The Ghost Who Never Was." *New Hampshire Profiles*, November 1968.

———. "Ocean Born Mary Yarn Is Fantasy." *Peterborough Transcript*, July 6, 1967.

Roy, L.M.A. *Ocean-Born Mary: A Romance*. Henniker, NH: self-published, 1935.

Sanders, Richard. *If a Pirate I Must Be: The True Story of Bartholomew Roberts, King of the Caribbean*. London: Aurum, 2007.

Schlosser, S.E. *Spooky New England*. Guilford, CT: Globe Pequot Press, 2004.

Schmidtchen, Ferne, ed. *The History of Londonderry*. Vol. 3. Londonderry, NH: Londonderry Town History Committee, 1977.

Smith, Susy. *Prominent American Ghosts*. Cleveland, OH: World Publishing, 1967.

Snow, Edward Rowe. *Legends of the New England Coast*. New York: Dodd, Mead & Company, 1957.

———. *Supernatural Mysteries and Other Tales*. New York: Dodd, Mead & Company, 1974.

Speare, Eva A., ed. *New Hampshire Folk Tales*. Charlestown, NH: Old Fort No. 4 Associates, 1993, originally published 1932.

Stearns, Ezra S., ed. *Genealogical and Family History of the State of New Hampshire: A Record of the Achievements of Her People in the Making of a Commonwealth and the Founding of a Nation*. New York: Lewis, 1908.

Steiger, Brad. *Real Ghosts, Restless Spirits and Haunted Minds*. New York: Award Books, 1968.

Thaxter, Celia. *Among the Isles of Shoals*. Boston, MA: J.R. Osgood, 1873.

Tolles, Bryant F., Jr., with Carolyn K. Tolles. *New Hampshire Architecture: An Illustrated Guide*. Hanover: New Hampshire Historical Society, 1979.

Ulrich, Laurel Thatcher. *The Age of Homespun: Objects and Stories in the Creation of an American Myth*. New York: Vintage, 2001.

Watson, John L., ed. *Memoirs of the Marstons of Salem*. Boston, MA: David Clapp and Son, 1873.

Webb, James. *Born Fighting: How the Scots-Irish Shaped America*. New York: Random House, 2005.

Weeks, Lyman Howard, ed., and Edwin M. Bacon. *An Historical Digest of the Provincial Press*. Boston, MA: Society for Americana, 1911.

Willey, George Franklyn, ed. *Willey's Book of Nutfield; a History of That Part of New Hampshire Comprised Within the Limits of the Old Township of Londonderry, from its Settlement in 1719 to the Present Time*. Derry Depot, NH: self-published, 1895.

Wood, Maureen, and Ron Kolek. *A Ghost a Day*. Avon, MA: Adams Media, 2010.

Yankee. "Living in a Legend." September 1996.

ONLINE SOURCES

Broome, Fiona. "Ocean-Born Mary of Henniker, NH, One of America's Most Famous Ghosts." www.hollowhill.com/nh/oceanborn1.htm.

Greer, Kathy. "Ocean Born Mary and Ghosts—Taking 'The Road Less Traveled.'" www.thegavel.net/Junlead1.html.

Londonderry, New Hampshire. "Ocean Born Mary, a Londonderry Halloween Tale." www.londonderrynh.net/?tag=ocean-born-mary-house.

Marin, Virginia. "Ocean-Born Mary Fulton: A Family Folktale." www.suite101.com/article.cfm/folklore/9264.

Robinson, J. Dennis. "The Truth About Ocean Born Mary." www.seacoastnh.com/arts/please042101.html.

ABOUT THE AUTHOR

Jeremy D'Entremont is a writer, photographer and tour guide whose specialty is New England maritime history. He is the author of nine books, including *The Lighthouses of Maine*, *Great Shipwrecks of the Maine Coast* and *The Lighthouse Handbook: New England*. He's written more than three hundred articles on lighthouses and maritime history, and his photographs have appeared in countless books, magazines and calendars. He's the historian and president of the American Lighthouse Foundation and founder of Friends of Portsmouth Harbor Lighthouses. He has appeared on the History Channel, public television, Travel Channel, Syfy Channel, WCVB-TV, WMUR-TV and has been heard on National Public Radio speaking about lighthouses and maritime history. His website on New England lighthouses, www.lighthouse.cc, was launched in 1997. Jeremy also offers tours based in Portsmouth, New Hampshire; see www.newenglandlighthousetours.com. He has lectured on and narrated cruises all along the New England coast. He lives in Portsmouth with his wife, Charlotte Raczkowski, and their tuxedo cat, Evie.

Photo by John Whalen.

Visit us at

www.historypress.net